Bird Stories

Edith M. Patch

Alpha Editions

This edition published in 2021

ISBN : 9789355110336

Design and Setting By
Alpha Editions
www.alphaedis.com
Email - info@alphaedis.com

As per information held with us this book is in Public Domain.
This book is a reproduction of an important historical work. Alpha Editions
uses the best technology to reproduce historical work in the same manner
it was first published to preserve its original nature. Any marks or number
seen are left intentionally to preserve its true form.

Contents

I CHICK, D.D.	- 1 -
II THE FIVE WORLDS OF LARIE	- 10 -
FOOTNOTES:	- 17 -
III PETER PIPER	- 18 -
IV GAVIA OF IMMER LAKE	- 27 -
V EVE AND PETRO	- 36 -
VI UNCLE SAM	- 47 -
VII CORBIE	- 54 -
VIII ARDEA'S SOLDIER	- 66 -
IX THE FLYING CLOWN	- 73 -
FOOTNOTES:	- 81 -
X THE LOST DOVE	- 82 -
XI LITTLE SOLOMON OTUS	- 89 -
FOOTNOTES:	- 97 -
XII BOB THE VAGABOND	- 98 -
NOTES	- 107 -
CONSERVATION	- 107 -

I
CHICK, D.D.

Right in the very heart of Christmas-tree Land there was a forest of firs that pointed to the sky as straight as steeples. A hush lay over the forest, as if there were something very wonderful there, that might be meant for you if you were quiet and waited for it to come. Perhaps you have felt like that when you walked down the aisle of a church, with the sun shining through the lovely glass in the windows. Men have often called the woods "temples"; so there is, after all, nothing so very strange in having a preacher live in the midst of the fir forest that grew in Christmas-tree Land.

And the sermon itself was not very strange, for it was about peace and good-will and love and helping the world and being happy—all very proper things to hear about while the bells in the city churches, way, way off, were ringing their glad messages from the steeples.

But the minister was a queer one, and his very first words would have made you smile. Not that you would have laughed at him, you know. You would have smiled just because he had a way of making you feel happy from the minute he began.

He sat on a small branch, and looked down from his pulpit with a dear nod of his little head, which would have made you want to cuddle him in the hollow of your two hands.

Firs that pointed to the sky.

His robe was of gray and white and buff-colored feathers, and he wore a black-feather cap and bib.

He began by singing his name. "Chick, D.D.," he called. Now, when a person has "D.D." written after his name, we have a right to think that he is trying to live so wisely that he can teach us how to be happier, too. Of course Minister Chick had not earned those letters by studying in college, like most parsons; but he had learned the secret of a happy heart in his school in the woods.

Yes, he began his service by singing his name; but the real sermon he preached by the deeds he did and the life he lived. So, while we listen to his happy song, we can watch his busy hours, until we are acquainted with the little black-capped minister who called himself "Chick, D.D."

Chick's Christmas-trees were decorated, and no house in the whole world had one lovelier that morning than the hundreds that were all about him as far as he could see. The dark-green branches of the pines and cedars had held themselves out like arms waiting to be filled, and the snow had been dropped on them in fluffy masses, by a quiet, windless storm. It had been very soft and lovely that way—a world all white and green below, with a sky of wonderful blue that the firs pointed to like steeples. Then, as if that were not decoration enough, another storm had come, and had put on the glitter that was brightest at the edge of the forest where the sun shone on it. The second storm had covered the soft white with dazzling ice. It had swept across the white-barked birch trees and their purple-brown branches, and had left them shining all over. It had dripped icicles from the tips of all the twigs that now shone in the sunlight brighter than candles, and tinkled like little bells, when the breezes clicked them together, in a tune that is called, "Woodland Music after an Ice-Storm."

"Woodland Music after an Ice-Storm."

That is the tune that played all about the black-capped bird as he flitted out of the forest, singing, "Chick, D.D.," as he came. The clear cold air and the exercise of flying after his night's sleep had given Chick a good healthy appetite, and he had come out for his breakfast.

He liked eggs very well, and there were, as he knew, plenty of them on the birch trees, for many a time he had breakfasted there. Eggs with shiny black shells, not so big as the head of a pin; so wee, indeed, that it took a hundred of them or more to make a meal for even little Chick.

But he wasn't lazy. He didn't have to have eggs cooked and brought to his table. He loved to hunt for them, and they were never too cold for him to relish; so out he came to the birch trees, with a cheery "Chick, D.D.," as if he were saying grace for the good food tucked here and there along the branches.

When he alighted, though, it wasn't the bark he found, but a hard, thick coating of ice. The branches rattled together as he moved among them and the icicles that dangled down rang and clicked as they struck one another. The ice-storm had locked in Chick's breakfast eggs, and, try as he would with his little beak, he couldn't get through to find them.

So Chick's Christmas Day began with hardship: for, though he sang gayly through the coldest weather, he needed food to keep him strong and warm. He was not foolish enough to spend his morning searching through the icy birch trees, for he had a wise little brain in his head and soon found out that it was no use to stay there. But he didn't go back to the forest and mope about it. Oh, no. Off he flew, down the short hill slope, seeking here and there as he went.

Where the soil was rocky under the snow, some sumachs grew, and their branches of red berries looked like gay Christmas decorations. The snow that had settled heavily on them had partly melted, and the soaked berries had stained it so that it looked like delicious pink ice-cream. Some of the stain had dripped to the snow below, so there were places that looked like pink ice-cream there, too. Then the ice-storm had crusted it over, and now it was a beautiful bit of bright color in the midst of the white-and-green-and-blue Christmas.

Chick stopped hopefully at the sumach bushes, not because he knew anything about ice-cream or cared a great deal about the berries; but sometimes there were plump little morsels hidden among them, that he liked to pull out and eat. If there was anything there that morning, though, it was locked in under the ice; and Chick flew on to the willows that showed where the brook ran in summer.

Ah, the willow cones! Surely they would not fail him! He would put his bill in at the tip and down the very middle, and find a good tasty bit to start with, and then he would feel about in other parts of the cone for small insects, which often creep into such places for the winter. The flight to the willows was full of courage. Surely there would be a breakfast there for a hungry Chick!

But the ice was so heavy on the willows that it had bent them down till the tips lay frozen into the crust below.

So from pantry to pantry Chick flew that morning, and every single one of them had been locked tight with an icy key. The day was very cold. Soon after the ice-storm, the mercury in the thermometer over at the Farm-House had dropped way down below the zero mark, and the wind was in the north. But the cold did not matter if Chick could find food. His feet were bare; but that did not matter, either, if he could eat. Nothing mattered to the brave little black-capped fellow, except that he was hungry, oh, so hungry! and he had heard no call from anywhere to tell him that any other bird had found a breakfast, either.

No, the birds were all quiet, and the distant church-bells had stopped their chimes, and the world was still. Still, except for the click of the icicles on the twigs when Chick or the wind shook them.

Then, suddenly, there was a sound so big and deep that it seemed to fill all the space from the white earth below to the blue sky above. A roaring BOOOOOOOM, which was something like the waves rushing against a rocky shore, and something like distant thunder, and something like the noise of a great tree crashing to the earth after it has been cut, and something like the sound that comes before an earthquake.

It is not strange that Chick did not know that sound. No one ever hears anything just like it, unless he is out where the snow is very light and very deep and covered with a crust.

Then, if the crust is broken suddenly in one place, it may settle like the top of a puffed-up pie that is pricked; and the air that has been prisoned under the crust is pushed out with a strange and mighty sound.

So that big BOOOOOOOM meant that something had broken the icy crust which, a moment before, had lain over the soft snow, all whole, for a mile one way and a mile another way, and half a mile to the Farm-House.

Yes, there was the Farmer Boy coming across the field, to the orchard that stood on the sandy hillside near the fir forest. He was walking on snowshoes, which cracked the crust now and then; and twice on the way to the orchard he heard a deep BOOOOOOOM, which he loved just as much as he loved the silence of the field when he stopped to listen now and then. For the winter sounds were so dear to the Farmer Boy who lived at the edge of Christmas-tree Land, that he would never forget them even when he should become a man. He would always remember the snowshoe tramps across the meadow; and in after years, when his shoulders held burdens he could not see, he would remember the bulky load he carried that morning without minding the weight a bit; for it was a big bag full of Christmas gifts, and the more heavily it pressed against his shoulder, the lighter his heart felt.

When he reached the orchard, he dropped the bag on the snow and opened it. Part of the gifts he spilled in a heap near the foot of a tree, and the rest he tied here and there to the branches. Then he stood still and whistled a clear sweet note that sounded like "Fee-bee."

Now, Chick, over by the willows had not known what BOOOOOOOM meant, for that was not in his language. But he understood "Fee-bee" in a minute, although it was not nearly so loud. For those were words he often used himself. They meant, perhaps, many things; but always something pleasant. "Fee-bee" was a call he recognized as surely as one boy recognizes the signal whistle of his chum.

So, of course, Chick flew to the orchard as quickly as he could and found his present tied fast to a branch. The smell of it, the feel of it, the taste of it, set him wild with joy. He picked at it with his head up, and sang "Chick, D.D." He picked at it with his head down and called, "Chick, D.D.D.D.D.D.D., Chick, D.D." He flew here and there, too gay with happiness to stay long anywhere, and found presents tied to other branches, too. At each one he sang "Chick, D.D., Chick, D.D.D.D. Dee Deee Deeee." It was, "indeed" the song of a hungry bird who had found good rich suet to nibble.

The Farmer Boy smiled when he heard it, and waited, for he thought others would hear it, too. And they did. Two birds with black-feather cap and bib heard it and came; and before they had had time to go frantic with delight and song, three others just like them came, and then eight more, and by that time there was such a "Chick"-ing and "D.D."-ing and such a whisking to and fro of black caps and black bibs, that no one paid much attention when Minister Chick, D.D., himself, perched on a branch for a minute, and gave the sweetest little warble that was ever heard on a winter's day. Then he whistled "Fee-bee" very clearly, and went to eating again, heeding the Farmer Boy no more than if he were not there at all.

And he wasn't there very long; for he was hungry, too; and that made him think about the good whiff he had smelled when he went through the kitchen with the snowshoes under his arm, just before he strapped them over his moccasins outside the door.

Yes, that was the Farmer Boy going away with a clatter over the snow-crust; but who were these coming through the air, with jerky flight, and with a jerky note something like "Twitterty-twit-twitterty-twit-twitterty-twitterty-twitterty-twit"? They flew like goldfinches, and they sounded like goldfinches, both in the twitterty song of their flight and their "Tweeet" as they called one another. But they were not goldfinches. Oh, my, no! For they were dressed in gray, with darker gray stripes at their sides; and when they scrambled twittering down low enough to show their heads in the sunlight, they could be seen to be wearing the loveliest of crimson caps, and some of them had rosy breasts.

The redpolls had come! And they found on top of the snow a pile of dusty sweepings from the hay-mow, with grass-seeds in it and some cracked corn and crumbs. And there were squash-seeds, and sunflower-seeds, and seedy apple-cores that had been broken up in the grinder used to crunch bones for the chickens; and there were prune-pits that had been cracked with a hammer.

The joy-songs of the birds over the suet and seeds seemed a signal through the countryside; and before long others came, too.

Among them there was a black-and-white one, with a patch of scarlet on the back of his head, who called, "Ping," as if he were speaking through his nose. There was one with slender bill and bobbed-off tail, black cap and white breast, grunting, "Yank yank," softly, as he ate.

But there was none to come who was braver or happier than Chick, D.D., and none who sang so gayly. After that good Christmas feast he and his flock returned each day; and when, in due time, the ice melted from the branches, it wasn't just suet they ate. It was other things, too.

That is how it happened that when, early in the spring, the Farmer Boy examined the apple-twigs, to see whether he should put on a nicotine spray for the aphids and an arsenical spray for the tent caterpillars, he couldn't find enough aphids to spray or enough caterpillars, either. Chick, D.D. and his flock had eaten their eggs.

Again, late in the summer, when it was time for the yellow-necked caterpillars, the red-humped caterpillars, the tiger caterpillars, and the rest of the hungry crew, to strip the leaves from the orchard, the Farmer Boy walked among the rows, to see how much poison he would need to buy for the August spray. And again he found that he needn't buy a single pound. Chick, D.D. and his family were tending his orchard!

Yes, Minister Chick was a servant in the good world he lived in. He saved leaves for the trees, he saved rosy apples for city girls and boys to eat, and he saved many dollars in time and spray-money for the Farmer Boy.

And all he charged was a living wage: enough suet in winter to tide him over the icy spells, and free house-rent in the old hollow post the Farmer Boy had nailed to the trunk of one of the apple trees.

That old hollow post was a wonderful home. Chick, D.D. had crept into it for the first time Christmas afternoon, when he had eaten until dusk overtook him before he had time to fly back to the shelter of the fir forest. He found that he liked that post. Its walls were thick and they kept out the wind; and, besides, was it not handy by the suet?

In the spring he liked it for another reason, too—the best reason in the world. It gave great happiness to Mrs. Chick. "Fee-bee?" he had asked her as he called her attention to it; and "Fee-bee," she had replied on looking it over. So he said, "Chick, D.D." in delight, and then perched near by, while he warbled cosily a brief song jumbled full of joy.

Chick and his mate had indeed chosen well, for it is a poor wall that will not work both ways. If the sides of the hollow post had been thick enough to keep out the coldest of the winter cold, they were also thick enough to keep out the hottest of the summer heat. If they kept out the wet of the driving storm, they held enough of the old-wood moisture within so that the room did not get too dry. Of course, it needed a little repair. But, then, what greater fun than putting improvements into a home? Especially when it can be done by the family, without expense!

So Mr. and Mrs. Chick fell to work right cheerily, and dug the hole deeper with their beaks. They didn't leave the chips on the ground before their doorway, either. They took them off to some distance, and had no heap near by, as a sign to say, "A bird lives here." For, sociable as they were all winter, they wanted quiet and seclusion within the walls of their own home.

And such a home it was! After it had been hollowed to a suitable depth, Chick had brought in a tuft of white hair that a rabbit had left among the brambles. Mrs. Chick had found some last year's thistle-down and some this year's poplar cotton, and a horse-hair from the lane. Then Chick had picked up a gay feather that had floated down from a scarlet bird that sang in the tree-tops, and tore off silk from a cocoon. So, bit by bit, they gathered their treasures, until many a woodland and meadow creature and plant had had a share in the softness of a nest worthy of eight dear white eggs with reddish-brown spots upon them. It was such a soft nest, in fact, with such dear eggs in it, that Chick brooded there cosily himself part of the time, and was happy to bring food to his mate when she took her turn.

In eleven or twelve days from the time the eggs were laid, there were ten birds in that home instead of two. The fortnight that followed was too busy for song. Chick and his mate looked the orchard over even more thoroughly than the Farmer Boy did; and before those eight hungry babies of theirs were ready to leave the nest, it began to seem as if Chick had eaten too many insect eggs in the spring, there were so few caterpillars hatching out. But the fewer there were, the harder they hunted; and the harder they hunted, the scarcer became the caterpillars. So when Dee, Chee, Fee, Wee, Lee, Bee, Mee, and Zee were two weeks old, and came out of the hollow post to seek their own living, the whole family had to take to the birches until a new crop of insect eggs had been laid in the orchard. This was no hardship. It only added the zest of travel and adventure to the pleasure of the days. Besides, it isn't just orchards that Chick, D.D. and his kind take care of. It is forests and shade-trees, too.

Hither and yon they hopped and flitted, picking the weevils out of the dead tips of the growing pine trees, serving the beech trees such a good turn that the beechnut crop was the heavier for their visit, doing a bit for the maple-sugar trees, and so on through the woodland.

Not only did they mount midget guard over the mighty trees, but they acted as pilots to hungry birds less skillful than themselves in finding the best feeding-places. "Chick, D.D.D.D.D.," they called in thanksgiving, as they found great plenty; and warblers and kinglets and creepers and many a bird beside knew the sound, and gathered there to share the bountiful feast that Chick, D.D. had discovered.

The gorgeous autumn came, the brighter, by the way, for the leaves that Chick had saved. The Bob-o-links, in traveling suits, had already left for the prairies of Brazil and Paraguay, by way of Florida and Jamaica. The strange honk of geese floated down from V-shaped flocks, as if they were calling, "Southward Ho!" The red-winged blackbirds gave a wonderful farewell chorus. Flock by flock and kind by kind, the migrating birds departed.

WHY?

Well, never ask Chick, D.D. The north with its snows is good enough for him. Warblers may go and nuthatches may come. 'Tis all one to Chick. He is not a bird to follow fashions others set.

This bird-of-the-happy-heart has courage to meet the coldest day with a joyous note of welcome. The winter is cheerier for his song. And, as you have guessed, it is not by word alone that he renders service. The trees of the north are the healthier for his presence. Because of him, the purse of man is fatter, and his larder better stocked. He has done no harm as harm is counted in the world he lives in. It is written in books that, in all the years, not one crime, not even one bad habit, is known of any bird who has called himself "Chick, D.D."

Because the world is always better for his living in it; and because no one can watch the black-capped sprite without catching, for a moment at least, a message of cheer and courage and service, does he not name himself rightly a minister?

Yes, surely, the little parson who dwells in the heart of Christmas-tree Land has a right to his "D.D.," even though he did not earn it in a college of men.

II
THE FIVE WORLDS OF LARIE

Larie was all alone in a little world. He had lived there many days, and had spent the time, minute by minute and hour by hour, doing nothing at all but growing. That one thing he had done well. There is no doubt about that; for he had grown from a one-celled little beginning of life into a creature so big that he filled the whole of his world crammed full. It was smooth, and it was hard, and its sides were curved around and about him so tightly that he could not even stretch his legs. There was no door. Larie was a prisoner. The prison-walls of his world held him so fast that he could not budge. That is, he could not budge anything but his head. He could move that a little.

Now, that is what we might call being in a fairly tight place. But you don't know Larie if you think he could not get out of it. There are few places so tight that we can't get out of them if we go about it the right way, and make the best of what power we have. That is just what Larie did. He had power to move his head enough to tap, with his beak, against the wall of his world that had become his prison. So he kept tapping with his beak. On the end of it was a queer little knob. With this he knocked against the hard smooth wall.

"Tap! tip tip!" went Larie's knob. Then he would rest, for it is not easy work hammering and pounding, all squeezed in so tight. But he kept at it again and again and again. And then at last he cracked his prison-wall; and lo, it was not a very thick wall after all! No thicker than an eggshell!

That is the way with many difficulties. They seem so very hard at first, and so very hopeless, and then end by being only a way to something very, very pleasant.

So here was Larie in his second world. Its thin, soft floor and its thick, soft sides were made of fine bright-green grass, which had turned yellowish in drying. It had no roof. The sun shone in at the top. The wind blew over. There had been no sun or wind in his eggshell world. It was comfortable to have them now. They dried his down and made it fluffy. There was plenty of room for its fluffiness. He could stretch his legs, too, and could wiggle his wings against his sides. This felt good. And he could move his head all he cared to. But he did not begin thumping the sides of his new world with it. He tucked it down between two warm little things close by, and went to sleep. The two warm little things were his sister and brother, for Larie was not alone in his nest-world.

The sun went down and the wind blew cold and the rain beat hard from the east; but Larie knew nothing of all this. A roof had settled down over his world while he napped. It was white as sea foam, and soft and dry and, oh, so very cosy, as it spread over him. The roof to Larie's second world was his mother's breast.

The storm and the night passed, and the sun and the fresh spring breeze again came in at the top of the nest. Then something very big stood near and made a shadow, and Larie heard a strange sound. The something very big was his mother, and the strange sound was her first call to breakfast. When Larie heard that, he opened his mouth. But nothing went into it. His brother and sister were being fed. He had never had any food in his mouth in all the days of his life. To be sure, his egg-world was filled with nourishment that he had taken into his body and had used in growing; but he had never done anything with his beak except to knock with the knob at the end of it against the shell when he pipped his way out. What a handy little knob that had been—just right for tapping. But, now that there was no hard wall about him to break, what should he use it for? Well, nothing at all; for the joke of it is, there was no knob there. It had dropped off, and he could never have another.

Never mind: he could open his beak just as well without it; and by-and-by his mother came again with a second call for breakfast, and that time Larie got his share. After that, there were calls for luncheon and for dinner, and luncheon again between that and supper; and part of the calls were from Mother and part from Father Gull.

Larie's second world, it seems, was a place where he and his brother and sister were hungry and were fed. This is a world in which dwell, for a time, all babies, whether they have two legs, like you and Larie, or four, like a pig with a curly tail, or six, like Nata who lived in Shanty Creek.[1] An important world it is, too; for health and strength and growing up, all depend upon it.

There was, however, only a rim of soft fine dry grass to show where Larie's nest-world left off and his third world began. So it is not surprising that, as soon as their legs were strong enough, Larie and his brother and sister stepped abroad; for what baby does not creep out of his crib as soon as ever he can?

They could not, for all this show of bravery, feed themselves like the sons of Peter Pan, or swim the waters like Gavia's two Olairs at Immer Lake. However grown up the three youngsters may have felt when they began to walk, Father and Mother Gull made no mistake about the matter, but fed them breakfasts, dinners, and suppers, and stuffed them so full of luncheons between meals, that the greedy little things just had to grow, so as to be able to swallow all that was brought them.

There were times, certainly, when Larie still felt very much a baby, even though he ran about nimbly enough. For instance, when he made a mistake and asked some gull, that was not his father or mother, for food, and got a rough beating instead of what he begged for!

Oh, then he felt like a forlorn little baby, indeed; for it was not pleasant to be whipped, and that sometimes cruelly, when he didn't know any better; for all the big gulls looked alike, with their foam-white bodies and their pearl-gray capes, and they were all bringing food; so how could he know who were and who were not his Father and Mother Gull? Well, he must learn to be careful, that was all, and stay where his very own could find and feed him; for gulls can waste no time on the young of other gulls—their own keep them busy enough, the little greedies!

Again, Larie must have felt very wee and helpless whenever a big man walked that way, shaking the ground with his heavy step and making a dark shadow as he came. Then, oh, then, Larie was a baby, and hid near a tuft of grass or between two stones, tucking his head out of sight, and keeping quite still as an ostrich does, or,—yes,—as perhaps a shy young human does, who hides his head in the folds of his mother's skirt when a stranger asks him to shake hands.

But few men trod upon Larie's island-world, and no man came to do him harm; for *the regulations under the Migratory-Bird Treaty Act prohibit throughout the United States the killing of gulls at any time.* That means that the laws of our country protect the gull, as of course you will understand, though Larie knew nothing about the matter.

Yes, think of it! There was a law, made at Washington in the District of Columbia, which helped take care of little downy Larie way off in the north on a rocky island.

I said "helped take care of"; for no law, however good it may be, can more than help make matters right. There has to be, besides, some sort of policeman to stand by the law and see that it is obeyed.

So Larie, although he never knew that, either, had a policeman; and the law and the policeman together kept him quite safe from the dangers which not many years ago most threatened the gulls on our coast islands. In those days, before there were gull-laws and gull-policemen, people came to the nests and took their eggs, which are larger than hens' eggs and good to eat; and people came, too, and killed these birds for their feathers. Then it was that the beautiful stiff wing-feathers, which should have been spread in flight, were worn upon the hats of women; and the soft white breast-feathers, which should have been brooding brownish eggs all spattered over with pretty marks, were stuffed into feather-beds for people to sleep on.

Well it was for Larie that he lived when he did; for his third world was a wonderful place and it was right that he should enjoy it in safety. When Larie first left his nest and went out to walk, he stepped upon a shelf of reddish rock, and the whole wall from which his shelf stuck out was reddish rock, too. Beyond, the rocks were greenish, and beyond that they were gray. Oh! the reddish and greenish and grayish rocks were beautiful to see when the fog lifted and the sun shone on them.

But Larie's island-world was not all rock of different colors: for over there, not too far away to see, was a dark-green spruce tree. Because rough winds had swept over this while it was growing, its branches were scraggly and twisted. They could not grow straight and even, like a tree in a quiet forest. But never think, for all of that, that Larie's spruce was not good to look upon. There is something splendid about a tree which, though bending to the will of the mighty winds that work their force upon it, grows sturdy and strong in spite of all. Such trees are somehow like boys and girls, who meet hardships with such courage when they are young, that they grow strong and sturdy of spirit, and warm of heart, with the sort of mind that can understand trouble in the world, and so think of ways to help it.

Birds, too, that had lived in rough winds.

Yes, perhaps Larie's tree was an emblem of courage. However that may be, it was a favorite spot on the island. Often it could be seen, that dark, rugged tree, which had battled with winds from its seedling days and grown victoriously, with three white gulls resting on its squarish top—birds, too, that had lived in rough winds and had grown strong in their midst.

There was more on the island than rocks and trees. Over much of it lay a carpet of grass. Soft and fine and vivid green it was, of the kind that had been gathered for Larie's nest and had turned yellowish in drying. Under the carpet, in underground lanes as long as a man's long arm, lived Larie's young neighbor-folk—little petrels, sometimes called "Mother Carey's Chickens."

There was even more on the island yet: for high on the rocks stood a lighthouse; and the man who kept the signal lights in order was no other than Larie's policeman himself. A useful life he lived, saving ships of the sea by the power of light, and birds of the sea by the power of law.

So that was Larie's third world—an island with a soft rug of bright-green grass, and big shelfy rocks of red and green and gray, and rugged dark-green trees, with white gulls resting on the branches, and a lighthouse with its signal.

All around and about that island lay Larie's fourth world—the sea. When his great day for swimming came, he slipped off into the water; and after that it was his, whenever he wished—his to swim or float upon, the wide-away ocean reaching as far as any gull need care to swim or float.

All over and above the sea stretched Larie's fifth world—the air. When his great day for flying came, he rose against the breeze, and his wings took him into that high-away kingdom that lifted as far as any gull need care to fly.

Now that Larie could both swim and fly, he was large, and acted in many ways like an old gull; but the feathers of his body were not white, and he did not wear over his back and the top of his spread wings a pearl-gray mantle.

Nor was he given the garb of his father and mother for a traveling suit, that winter when he went south with the others, to a place where the Gulf Stream warmed the water whereon he swam and the air wherein he flew.

But there came a time when Larie had put off the clothes of his youth and donned the robe of a grown gull. And as he sailed in the breezes of his fifth world, which blew over the cold sea, and across the island with a carpet of green and rocks of red and green and gray,—for he was again in the North,—he was beautiful to behold, the flight of a gull being so wonderful that the heart of him who sees quickens with joy.

Larie was not alone. There were so many with him that, when they flew together in the distance, they looked as thick as snowflakes in the air; and when they screamed together, the din was so great that people who were not used to hearing them put their hands over their ears.

And more than that, Larie was not alone; for there sailed near him in the air and floated beside him in the sea another gull, at whom he did not scream, but to whom he talked pleasantly, saying, "me-you," in a musical tone that she understood.

Floated beside him in the sea another gull, to whom he talked pleasantly.

Larie and his mate found much to do that spring. One game that never failed to interest them was meeting the ships many, many waves out at sea, and following them far on their way. For on the ships were men who threw away food they could not use, and the gulls gathered in flocks to scramble and fight for this. Children on board the ships laughed merrily to see them, and tossed crackers and biscuits out for the fun of watching the hungry-birds come close, to feed.

Many a feast, too, the fishermen gave the gulls, when they sorted the contents of their nets and threw aside what they did not want.

Besides this, Larie and his mate and their comrades picnicked in high glee at certain harbors where garbage was left; for gulls are thrifty folk and do not waste the food of the world.

From their feeding habits you will know that these beautiful birds are scavengers, eating things which, if left on the sea or shore, would make the water foul and the air impure. Thus it is that Nature gives to a scavenger the duty of service to all living creatures; and the freshness of the ocean and the cleanness of the sands of the shore are in part a gift of the gulls, for which we should thank and protect them.

Relish as they might musty bread and mouldy meat, Larie and his mate enjoyed, too, the sport of catching fresh food; and many a clam hunt they had in true gull style. They would fly above the water near the shore, and when they were twenty or thirty feet high, would plunge down head-first. Then they would poke around for a clam, with their heads and necks under water and their wings out and partly unfolded, but not flopping; and a comical sight they were!

After Larie found a clam, he would fly high into the air a hundred feet or so, and then drop it.

It was not for food alone that Larie and his mate lived that spring.

After Larie found a clam, he would fly high into the air a hundred feet or so above the rocks, and then, stretching way up with his head, drop the clam from his beak. Easily, with wings fluttering slightly, Larie would follow the clam, floating gracefully, though quickly, down to where it had cracked upon the rocks. The morsel in its broken shell was now ready to eat, for Larie and his mate did not bake their sea-food or make it into chowder. Cold salad flavored with sea-salt was all they needed.

Exciting as were these hunts with the flocks of screaming gulls, it was not for food alone that Larie and his mate lived that spring. For under the blue of the airy sky there was an ocean, and in that ocean there was an island, and on that island there was a nest, and in that nest there was an egg—the first that the mate of Larie had ever laid. And in that egg was a growing gull, their eldest son—a baby Larie, alone inside his very first world.

FOOTNOTES:

[1] *Hexapod Stories*, page 80.

III
PETER PIPER

One was named Sandy, because Sandy is a Scotch name and there were bluebells growing on the rocks; so it seemed right that one of them should have a Scotch name, and what could be better, after all, than Sandy for a sandpiper? One was named Pan, because he piped sweetly among the reeds by the river. One, who came out of his eggshell before his brothers, was named Peter, for his father.

But Mother Piper never called her children Sandy and Pan and Peter. She called them all "Pete." She was so used to calling her mate "Pete," that that name was easier than any other for her to say.

The three of them played by the river all day long. Each amused himself in his own way and did not bother his brothers, although they did not stray too far apart to talk to one another. This they did by saying, "Peep," now and then.

About once an hour, and sometimes oftener, Mother Piper came flying over from Faraway Island, crying, "Pete, Pete, Pete," as if she were worried. It is no wonder that she was anxious about Sandy and Peter and Pan, for, to begin with, she had had four fine children, and the very first night they were out of their nest, the darlings, a terrible prowling animal named Tom or Tabby had killed one of her babies.

One was named Peter, for his father.

But Peter and Pan and Sandy were too young to know much about being afraid. So they played by the river all day long, care-free and happy. Their sweet little voices sounded contented as they said, "Peep," one to another. Their queer little tails looked frisky as they went bob-bob-bob-bing up and down every time they stepped, and sometimes when they didn't. Their dear little heads went forward and back in a merry sort of jerk. There were so many things to do, and every one of them a pleasure!

Oh! here was Sandy clambering up the rocky bank, so steep that there was roothold only for the blue-bells, with stems so slender that one name for them is "hair-bell." But Sandy did not fall. He tripped lightly up and about, with sure feet; and where the walking was too hard, he fluttered his wings and flew to an easier place. Once he reached the top of the bank, where the wild roses were blossoming. And wherever he went, and wherever he came, he found good tasty insects to eat; so he had picnic-luncheons all along the way.

Ho! here was Pan wandering where the river lapped the rocky shore. His long slender legs were just right for wading, and his toes felt comfortable in the cool water. There was a pleasing scent from the sweet-gale bushes, which grew almost near enough to the river to go wading, too; and there was a spicy smell when he brushed against the mint, which wore its blossoms in pale purple tufts just above the leaves along the stem. And every now and then, whether he looked at the top of the water or at the rocks on the shore-edge, he found tempting bits of insect game to eat as he waded along.

Oho! here was Peter on an island as big as an umbrella, with a scooped-out place at one side as deep as the hollow in the palm of a man's hand. This was shaped exactly right for Peter's bathtub, and as luck would have it, it was filled to the brim with water. Such a cool splashing—once, twice, thrice, with a long delightful flutter; and then out into the warm sunshine, where the feathers could be puffed out and dried! These were the very first real feathers he had ever had, and he hadn't had them very long; and my, oh, my! but it was fun running his beak among them, and fixing them all fine, like a grown-up bird. And when he was bathed and dried, there was a snack to eat near by floating toward him on the water.

Oh! Ho! and Oho! it was a day to be gay in, with so many new amusements wherever three brave, fearless little sandpipers might stray.

Then came sundown; and in the pleasant twilight Peter and Pan and Sandy somehow found themselves near each other on the bank, still walking forth so brave and bold, and yet each close enough to his brothers to hear a "Peep," were it ever so softly whispered.

Did it just happen that about that time Mother Piper came flying low over the water from Faraway Island to Nearby Island, calling, "Pete, Pete, Pete," in a different tone, a sort of sundown voice?

Was that the way to speak to three big, 'most-grown-up sandpiper sons, who had wandered about so free of will the livelong day?

Ah, but where were the 'most-grown-up sons? Gone with the sun at sundown; and, instead, there were three cosy little birds, with their heads still rumpled over with down that was not yet pushed off the ends of their real feathers, and a tassel of down still dangling from the tip of each funny tail.

And three dear, sweet, little voices answered, "Peep," every time Mother Piper called, "Pete"; and three little sons tagged obediently after her as she called them from place to place all round and all about Nearby Island, teaching them, perhaps, to make sure there was no Tabby and no Tommy on their camping-ground.

So it was that, after twilight, when darkness was at hand and the curfew sounded for human children to be at home, Peter and Pan and Sandy settled down near each other and near Mother Piper for the night.

And where was Peter Piper, who had been abroad the day long, paying little attention to his family? He, too, at nightfall, had come flying low from

Faraway Island; and now, with his head tucked behind his wing, was asleep not a rod away from Mother Piper and their three sons.

Somehow it was very pleasant to know that they were near together through the starlight—the five of them who had wandered forth alone by sunlight.

But not for long was the snug little Nearby Island to serve for a night camp. Mother Piper had other plans. Like the wise person she was, she let her children find out many things for themselves, though she kept in touch with them from time to time during the day, to satisfy herself that they were safe. And at night she found that they were willing enough to mind what they were told to do, never seeming to bother their heads over the fact that every now and then she led them to a strange camp-ground.

So they did not seem surprised or troubled when, one night soon, Mother Piper, instead of calling them to Nearby Island, as had been her wont, rested patiently in plain sight on a stump near the shore and, with never a word, waited for the sunset hour to reach the time of dusk. Then she flew to the log where Peter Piper had been teetering up and down, and what she said to him I do not know. But a minute later, back she flew, this time rather high overhead, and swooped down toward the little ones with a quick "Pete-weet." After her came Peter Piper flying, also rather high overhead, and swooping down toward his young. Then Mother and Peter Piper went in low, slow flight to Faraway Island.

Were they saying good-night to their babies? Were their sons to be left on the bank by themselves, now that they had shaken the last fringe of down from their tails and lost the fluff from their heads? Did they need no older company, now that they looked like grown-up sandpipers except that their vests had no big polka dots splashed over them?

Ah, no! At Mother Piper's "Pete-weet," Peter answered, "Peep," lifted his wings, and flew right past Nearby Island and landed on a rock on Faraway Island. And, "Peep," called Sandy, fluttering after. And, "Peep," said Pan, stopping himself in the midst of his teetering, and flying over Nearby Island on his way to the new camp-ground.

That is how it happened that they had their last luncheon on the shore of Faraway Island before snuggling down to sleep that night.

One of the haunts of Peter and Pan and Sandy was Cardinal-Flower Path. This lovely place was along the marshy shore not far from Nearby Island. It was almost white with the fine blooms of water-parsnip, an interesting plant from the top of its blossom head to the lowest of its queer under-water leaves. And here and there, among the lacy white, a stalk of a different sort grew, with red blossoms of a shade so rich that it is called the cardinal flower. Every now and then a ruby-throated hummingbird darted quickly above the water-parsnips straight to the cardinal throat of the other flower, and found refreshment served in frail blossom-ware of the glorious color he loved best of all.

And it would be well for all children of men to know that, although three bright active children of sandpipers ran teetering about Cardinal-Flower Path many and many a day, the place was as lovely to look upon at sundown as at sunrise, for not one wonderful spray had been broken from its stem. So it happened, because the children who played there were Sandy and Peter and Pan, that the cardinal flowers lived their life as it was given them by Nature, serving refreshments for hummingbirds through the summer day, and setting seeds according to their kind for other cardinal flowers and other hummingbirds another year.

But even the charms of Cardinal-Flower Path did not hold Pan and Peter and Sandy many weeks. They seemed to be a sort of gypsy folk, with the love of wandering in their hearts; and it is pleasant to know that, as soon as they were grown enough, there was nothing to prevent their journeying forth with Peter and Mother Piper.

Of all the strange and wonderful plants and birds and insects they met upon the way I cannot tell you, for, in all my life, I have not traveled so far as these three children went long before they were one year old. They went, in fact, way to the land where the insects live that are so hard and beautiful and gemlike that people sometimes use them for jewels. These are called "Brazilian beetles," and you can tell by that name where the Pipers spent the winter, though it may seem a very far way for a young bird to go, with neither train nor boat to give him a lift.

Not even tired they were, from all accounts, those little feather-folk; and why, indeed, should they be tired? A jaunt from a northern country to Brazil was not too much for a healthy bird, with its sure breath and pure rich blood. There was food enough along the trail—they chose their route wisely enough for that, you may be sure; and they were in no great haste either going or coming.

"Coming," did I say? Why, surely! You didn't think those sandpipers *stayed* in Brazil? What did they care for green gem-like beetles, after all? The only decorations they ever wore were big dark polka dots on their vests. Perhaps they were all pleased with them, when their old travel-worn feathers dropped out and new ones came in. Who can tell? They had a way of running their bills through their plumage after a bath, as if they liked to comb their pretty feathers.

Be that as it may, there was something beneath their feathers that quickened like the heart of a journeying gypsy when, with nodding heads and teetering tails, they started again for the north.

Did they dream of a bank where the blue-bells grew, and a shore spiced with the fragrance of wild mint?

No one will ever know just how Nature whispers to the bird, "Northward ho!" But we know they come in the springtime, and right glad are we to hear their voices.

So Peter Piper, Junior, came back again to the shore of Nearby Island. And do you think Sandy and Pan walked behind him for company, calling, "Peep," one to another? And do you think Mother Piper and Father Peter showed him the way to Faraway Island at sun-down, and guarded him o' nights? Not they! They were busy, every one, with their own affairs, and Peter would just have to get along without them.

Well, Peter could—Peter and Dot. For of course he was a grown-up sandpiper now, with a mate of his own, nodding her wise little head the livelong day, and teetering for joy all over the rocks where the red columbine grew.

The spot she teetered to most of all.

The spot she teetered to most of all was a little cup-shaped hollow high up on the border of the ledge, where the sumachs were big as small trees and where the sweet fern scented the air. The hollow was lined tidily and softly with dried grass, and made a comfortable place to sit, no doubt. At least, Dot liked it; and Peter must have had some fondness for it, too, for he slipped on when Dot was not there herself. It just fitted their little bodies, and there were four eggs in it of which any sandpiper might well have been proud; for they were much, much bigger than most birds the size of Dot could ever lay. In fact, her little body could hardly have covered them snugly enough to keep them warm if they had not been packed just so, with the pointed ends pushed down into the middle of the rather deep nest.

The eggs were creamy white, with brown spots splashed over them—the proper sort of eggs (if only they had been smaller) to tuck beneath a warm breast decorated with pretty polka dots. But still, they must have been her very own, or Dot could not have taken such good care of them.

Because of this care, day by day the little body inside each shell grew from the wonderful single cell it started life with, to a many-celled creature, all fitted out with lungs and a heart and rich warm blood, and very slender legs, and very dear heads with very bright eyes, and all the other parts it takes to make a bird. When the birds were all made, they broke the shells and pushed aside the pieces. And four more capable little rascals never were hatched.

Why, almost before one would think they had had time to dry their down and stretch their legs and get used to being outside of shells instead of inside, those little babies walked way to the edge of the river, and from that time forth never needed their nest.

And look! the fluffy, cunning little dears are nodding their heads and teetering their tails! Yes, that proves that they must be sandpipers, even if we did have doubts of those eggs. Ah! Dot knew what she was about all along. The size of her eggs might fool a person, but she had not worried. Why, indeed, should she be troubled? Those big shells had held food-material enough, so that her young, when hatched, were so strong and well-developed that they could go wandering forth at once. They did not lie huddled in their nest, helplessly begging Peter Piper and Mother Dot to bring them food. Not they! Out they toddled, teetering along the shore, having picnics from the first—the little gypsy babies!

Tabby did not catch any of them, though one night she tried, and gave Dot an awful scare. It was while they were still tiny enough to be tucked under their mother's feathers after sundown, and before they could manage to get, stone by stone, to Nearby Island. So they were camped on the shore, and the prowling cat came very near. So near, in fact, that Mother Dot fluttered away from her young, calling back to them, in a language they understood, to scatter a bit, and then lie so still that not even the green eyes of the cat could see a motion. The four little Pipers obeyed. Not one of them questioned, "Why, Mother?" or whined, "I don't want to," or whimpered, "I'm frightened," or boasted, "Pooh, there's nothing here."

Dot led the crouching enemy away by fluttering as if she had a broken wing, and she called for help with all the agony of her mother-love. "Pete," she cried, "Pete," and "Pete, Pete, Pete!"

No one who hears the wail of a frightened sandpiper begging protection for her young can sit unmoved.

Someone at the Ledge House heard Dot, and gave a low whistle and a quick command. Then there was a dashing rush through the bushes, that sounded as if a dog were chasing a cat. A few minutes later Dot's voice again called in the dark—this time, not in anguish of heart, but very cosily and gently. "Pete-weet?" she whispered; and four precious little babies murmured, "Peep," as they snuggled close to the spotted breast of their mother.

So it happened that two sons and two daughters of Peter Piper, Junior, played and picnicked and bathed by the river. The one who had first pipped his eggshell was named Peter the Third, for his father and his grandfather, and a finer young sandpiper never shook the fluff of down from his head or the fringe from his tail, when his real feathers pushed into their places.

What his brother and sisters were named, I never knew; and it didn't matter much, for their mother called them all "Pete."

Dallying happily along the river-edge.

Peter the Third and the others grew up as Pan and Peter and Sandy had grown, dallying happily along the river-edge, and as happily accepting the guidance of their mother, who made her slow flight from Faraway Island every now and then, usually so low that her spotted breast was reflected in the clear water as she came, the white markings in her wings showing above and below.

Of course, as soon as the season came for their migration journey, the four of them started cheerfully off with Peter and Dot, for a leisurely little flight to Brazil and back—to fill the days, as it were, with pleasant wanderings, from the time the hummingbird fed at the feast of the cardinal flower in late summer, until he should be hovering over the columbine in the spring.

IV
GAVIA OF IMMER LAKE

Once upon a time, it was four millions of years ago. There were no people then all the way from Florida to Alaska. There was, indeed, in all this distance, no land to walk upon, except islands in the west where the Rocky Mountains are now. That is the only place where the country that is now the United States of America stuck up out of the water. Everywhere else were the waves of the sea. There were no people, even on the Rocky Mountain Islands. None at all.

No, the creatures that visited those island shores in those old days were not people, but birds. Nearly as large as men they were, and they had teeth on their long slender jaws, and they had no wings. They came to the islands, perhaps, only at nesting-time; for their legs and feet were fitted for swimming and not walking, and they lived upon fish in the sea. So they dwelt, with no man to see them, on the water that stretched from sea to sea; and what their voices were like, no man knows.

A million years, perhaps, passed by, and then another million, and maybe another million still; and the birds without wings and with teeth were no more. In their places were other birds, much smaller—birds with wings and no teeth; but something like them, for all that: for their feet also were fitted for swimming and not walking, and they, too, visited the shore little, if at all, except at nesting-time, and they lived upon fish in the water.

And what their voices were like, all men may know who will go to the wilderness lakes and listen; for, wonderful as it may seem, these second birds have come down to us through perhaps a million years, and live to-day, giving a strange clear cry before a storm, and at other times calling weirdly in lone places, so that men who are within hearing always say, "The loons are laughing."

Gavia was a loon who had spent the winter of 1919-1920 on the Atlantic Ocean. There had hardly been, perhaps, in a million years a handsomer loon afloat on any sea. Even in her winter coat she was beautiful; and when she put on her spring suit, she was lovelier still.

She and her mate had enjoyed the sea-fishing and had joined a company of forty for swimming parties and other loon festivities; for life on the ocean waves has many interests, and there is never a lack of entertainment. The salt-water bathing, diving, and such other activities as the sea affords, were pleasant for them all. Then, too, the winter months made a chance for rest, a change from home-duties, and a freedom from looking out for the children, that gave the loons a care-free manner as they rode the waves far out at sea.

Immer Lake.

Considering all this, it seems strange, does it not, that when the spring of 1920 had gone no further than to melt the ice in the northern lakes, Gavia and her mate left the sea and took strong flight inland.

What made them go, I cannot explain. I do not understand it well enough. I do not really know what urges the salmon to leave the Atlantic Ocean in the spring and travel up the Penobscot or the St. John River. I never felt quite sure why Peter Piper left Brazil for the shore where the blue-bells nod. All I can tell you about it is that a feeling came over the loons that is called a migration instinct; and, almost before Gavia and her mate knew what was happening to them, they had flown far and far from the Ocean, and were laughing weirdly over the cold waters of Immer Lake.

The shore was dark with the deep green of fir trees, whose straight trunks had blisters on them where drops of fragrant balsam lay hidden in the bark. And here and there trees with white slender trunks leaned out over the water, and the bark on these peeled up like pieces of thin and pretty paper. Three wonderful vines trailed through the woodland, and each in its season blossomed into pink and fragrant bells. But what these were, and how they looked, is not a part of this story, for Gavia never wandered among them. Her summer paths lay upon and under the water of the lake, as her winter trails had been upon and under the water of the sea.

Ah, if she loved the water so, why did she suddenly begin to stay out of it? If she delighted so in swimming and diving and chasing wild wing-races over the surface, why did she spend the day quietly in one place?

Of course you have guessed it! Gavia was on her nest. She had hidden her two babies among the bulrushes for safety, and must stay there herself to keep them warm. They were not yet out of their eggshells, so the only care they needed for many a long day and night was constant warmth enough for growth. They lay near each other, the two big eggs, of a color that some might call brown and some might call green, with dark-brown spots splashed over them.

Two babies, not yet out of their eggshells, hidden among the rushes.

The nest Gavia and her mate had prepared for them was a heap of old wet reeds and other dead water-plants, which they had piled up among the stems of the rushes until it reached six inches or more out of the water. They were really in the centre of a nest island, with water all about them. So, you see, Gavia was within splashing distance of her fishing-pool after all.

She and her mate, indeed, were in the habit of making their nests here in the cove; though the two pairs of Neighbor Loons, who built year after year farther up the lake, chose places on the island near the water-line in the spring; and when the water sank lower later on, they were left high and dry where they had to flounder back and forth to and from the nest, as awkward on land as they were graceful in the water.

Faithful to her unhatched young as Gavia was, it is not likely that she alone kept them warm for nearly thirty days and nights; for Father Loon remained close at hand, and would he not help her with this task?

Gavia, sitting on her nest, did not look like herself of the early winter months when she had played among the ocean waves. For her head and neck were now a beautiful green, and she wore two white striped collars, while the back of her feather coat was neatly checked off with little white squarish spots. Father Loon wore the same style that she did. Summer and winter, they dressed alike.

Yes, a handsome couple, indeed, waited that long month for the birth of their twins, growing all this time inside those two strong eggshells. At last, however, the nest held the two babies, all feathered with down from the very first, black on their backs and gray shading into white beneath.

Did I say the nest held them? Well, so it did for a few hours. After that, they swam the waters of Immer Lake, and their nest was home no longer. Peter Piper's children themselves were not more quick to run than Gavia's twins were to swim and dive.

I think, perhaps, they were named Olair; for Gavia often spoke in a very soft mellow tone, saying, "Olair"; and her voice, though a bit sad, had a pleasing sound. So we will call them the two Olairs.

They were darlings, those baby loons, swimming about (though not very fast at first), and diving out of sight in the water every now and then (but not staying under very long at the beginning). Then, when they were tired or in a hurry, they would ride on the backs of Gavia and Father Loon: and they liked it fine, sailing over the water with no trouble at all, just as if they were in a boat, with someone else to do the rowing.

Oh, yes, they were darlings! Had you seen one of them, you could hardly have helped wanting to cuddle him. But do you think you could catch one, even the youngest? Not a bit of it. If you had given chase in a boat, the wee-est loon would have sailed off faster yet on the back of his father; and when you grew tired and stopped, you would have heard, as if mocking you, the old bird give, in a laughing voice, the *Tremble Song*:

"O, ha-ha-ha, ho!—O, ha-ha-ha, ho!—O, ha-ha-ha, ho!—O, ha-ha-ha, ho!—"

If you had tried again a few days later, the young loon would have been able to dive and swim by himself out of sight under water, the old ones giving him warning of danger and telling him what to do.

But no child chased the two Olairs and no lawbreaker fired a shot at Gavia or Father Loon. They had frights and narrow escapes in plenty without that; but those were of the sorts that loons get used to century after century, and not modern disasters, like guns, that people have recently brought into wild places. For the only man who dwelt on the shore of Immer Lake was a minister.

Because he loved his fellow men, this minister of Immer Lake spent part of his days among them, doing such service to the weak of spirit as only a minister can do, who has faith that there is some good in every person. At such times he was a sort of servant to all who needed him.

Because he loved, also, his fellow creatures who had lived in the beautiful wild places of this land much longer than any man whatsoever, he spent part of his days among them. At such times he was a sort of hermit.

Then no handy trolley rumbled by to take him on his near way. No train shrieked its departure to distant places where he might go. There was no interesting roar of mill or factory making things to use. There was no sociable tread of feet upon the pavement, to give him a feeling of human companionship.

But, for all that, it was not a silent world the minister found at Immer Lake. On sunny days the waves, touching the rocks on the shore, sang gently, "Bippo-bappo, bippo-bappo." The trees clapped their leaves together as the breezes bade them. The woodpeckers tapped tunes to each other on their hollow wooden drums. The squirrels chattered among the branches. At dawn and at dusk the thrushes made melodies everywhere about.

On stormy nights the waves slapped loudly upon the rocks. The branches whacked against one another at the mighty will of the wind. The thunder roared applause at the fireworks the lightning made. And best of all, like the very spirit of the wild event, there rang the strange, sweet moaning *Storm Song of the Loon*:—

"A-a-ah l-u-u-u-u-u-u´ la. A-a-ah l-u-u-u-u-u-u´ la. A-a-ah l-u-u-u-u-u-u´ la. A-a-ah l-u-u-u-u-u-u´ la."

The minister of Immer Lake liked that song, and he liked the other music that they made. So it was that he sat before his door through many a summer twilight, and played on his violin until the loons answered with the *Tremble Song*:—

"O, ha-ha-ha, ho! O, ha-ha-ha, ho! O, ha-ha-ha, ho! O, ha-ha-ha, ho!"

Then they would swim up and up, until they floated close to his cottage, feeding unafraid near by, while he played softly.

Often, when Gavia and her mate were resting there or farther up the lake, some other loon would fly over; and then Father Loon would throw his head way forward and give another sort of song. "Oh-a-lee'!" he would begin, with his bill wide open; and then, nearly closing his mouth, he would sing, "Cleo´-pe´´-a-rit´." The "Oh" starts low and then rises in a long, drawn way. Perhaps in all the music of Immer Lake there is nothing queerer than the *Silly Song of Father Loon*:—

"Oh-a-lee´! Cleo´-p´´-a-rit´, cleo´-pe´´-a-rit´, cleo´-per´´-wer-wer!Oh-a-lee´! Cleo´-p´´-a-rit´, cleo´-pe´´-a-rit´, cleo´-pe´´-wer-wer!"

Such were the songs the two Olairs heard often and again, while they were growing up; and they must have added much to the interest of their first summer.

Altogether they had endless pleasures, and were as much at ease in the water as if there were no more land near them than there had been near those other young birds that had teeth and no wings, four million years or so ago. Their own wings were still small and flipper-like when, about the first of August, they were spending the day, as they often did, in a small cove. They were now about two-thirds grown, and their feathers were white beneath and soft bright brown above, with bars of white spots at their shoulders. They had funny stiff little tails, which they stuck up out of the water or poked out of sight, as they wished. They swam about in circles, and preened their feathers with their bills, which were still small and gray, and not black like those of the old birds.

After a time Gavia came swimming toward them, all under water except her head. Suddenly Father Loon joined her, and they both began diving and catching little fishes for the two Olairs. For the vegetable part of their dinner they had shreds of some waterplant, which Gavia brought them, dangling from her bill. Surely never a fresher meal was served than fish just caught and greens just pulled! No wonder it was that the young loons grew fast, and were well and strong. After the twins were fed, Gavia and Father Loon sank from sight under the water, heads and all, and the Olairs saw no more of them for two hours or so, though they heard them now and then singing, sometimes the *Tremble Song* and sometimes the *Silly Song*.

They were good children, and did not try to tag along or sulk because they were left behind. First they dabbled about and helped themselves, for dessert, to some plant growing under water, gulping down rather large mouthfuls of it. Then they grew drowsy; and what could have been pleasanter than going to sleep floating, with the whole cove for a cradle?

You could never guess how those youngsters got ready for their nap. Just like a grown-up! Each Olair rolled over on one side, till the white under-part of his body showed above water. Then he waved the exposed leg in the air, and tucked it away, with a quick flip, under the feathers of his flank. Thus one foot was left in the water, for the bird to paddle with gently while he slept, so that he would not be drifted away by the wind. But that day one of the tired water-babies went so sound asleep that he didn't paddle enough, and the wind played a joke on him by shoving him along to the snaggy edge of the cove and bumping him against a log. That was a surprise, and he woke with a start and swam quickly back to the middle of the cove, where the other Olair was resting in the open water.

While their children were napping, Gavia and Father Loon went to a party. On the way, they stopped for a bit of fishing by themselves. Gavia began by suddenly flapping around in a big circle, slapping the water with wing-tips and feet, and making much noise as she spattered the spray all about. Then she quickly poked her head under water, as if looking for fish. Father Loon, who had waited a little way off, dived a number of times, as if to see what Gavia had scared in his direction.

While their children were napping, Gavia and Father Loon went to a party.

Then they both dove deep, and swam under water until they came near the four Neighbor Loons, who had left their two families of young dozing, and had also come out for a good time.

When Father Loon caught sight of his four neighbors, he sang the *Silly Song*, after which the six birds ran races on the water. They all started about the same time and went pell-mell in one direction, their feet and wings going as if they hardly knew whether to swim or fly, and ending by doing both at once. Then they would all stop, as suddenly as if one of them had given a signal, and turning, would dash in the opposite direction, racing to and fro again and again and again. Oh! it was a grand race, and there is no knowing how long they would have kept it up, had not something startled them so that they all stopped and sang the *Tremble Song*, which sounds like strange laughter. They opened their mouths quite wide and, wagging the lower jaw up and down with every "ha," they sang "O, ha-ha-ha, ho!" so many times that it seemed as if they would never get through. And, indeed, how could they tell when the song was ended, for every verse was like the one before?

Then all at once they stopped singing and began some flying stunts. A stiff breeze was blowing, and, facing this, they pattered along, working busily with wings and feet, until they could get up speed enough to leave the water and take to flight. Though it was rather a hard matter to get started, when they were once under way they flew wonderfully well, and the different pairs seemed to enjoy setting their wings and sailing close together around a large curve. They went so fast part of the time that, when they came down to the surface of the water again, they plunged along with a splash and ploughed a furrow in the water before they could come to a stop.

Of course, by that time they were hungry enough for refreshments! So Gavia went off to one side and stirred the water up as if she were trying to scare fish toward the others, who waited quietly. Then they all dived, and what their black sharp-pointed bills found under water tasted good to those hungry birds.

After that the loon party broke up, and each pair went to their own home cove, where they had left their young. It had been a pleasant way to spend the time sociably together; and loons like society very much, if they can select their own friends and have their parties in a wilderness lake. But gay and happy as they had been at their merrymaking, Gavia and her mate were not sorry to return to the two Olairs, who had long since wakened from their naps and were glad to see their handsome father and mother again.

By the time the two Olairs were full grown, Gavia had molted many of her prettiest feathers and was looking rather odd, as she had on part of her summer suit and part of her winter one. Father Loon had much the same appearance; for, of course, birds that live in the water cannot shed their feathers as many at a time as Corbie could, but must change their feather-wear gradually, so that they may always have enough on to keep their bodies dry. And summer and winter, you may be sure that a loon takes good care of his clothes, oiling them well to keep them waterproof.

Fall grew into winter, and the nest where Gavia had brooded the spring before now held a mound of snow in its lap. The stranded log against which the little Olair had been bumped while he was napping, months ago, was glazed over with a sparkling crust. The water where Gavia and Father Loon had fished for their children, and had played games and run races with Neighbor Loons, was sealed tight with a heavy cover of ice.

And it may be, if you should sail the seas this winter, that you will see the two Olairs far, far out upon the water. What made them leave the pleasures of Immer Lake just when they did, I cannot explain. I do not understand it well enough. I never felt quite sure why Peter Piper left the shore where the cardinal flowers glowed, for far Brazil. All I can tell you about it is that a feeling came over the loons that is called a migration instinct, and, almost before they knew what was happening to them, they were laughing weirdly through the ocean storms.

If you see them, you will know that they are strange birds whose ancestors reach back and back through the ages, maybe a million years. You will think—as who would not?—that a loon is a wonderful gift that Nature has brought down through all the centuries; a living relic of a time of which we know very little except from fossils men find and guess about.

It is small wonder their songs sound strange to our ears, for their voices have echoed through a world too old for us to know. It makes us a bit timid to think about all this, as it does the minister of Immer Lake, who sits before his door through many a summer twilight, playing on his violin until the loons answer him with their *Tremble Song*:—

"O, ha-ha-ha, ho! O, ha-ha-ha, ho!"

V
EVE AND PETRO

If swallows studied history, 1920 would have been an important date for Eve and Petro. It was the one hundredth anniversary of the year when a man named Long visited cliff swallows among the Rocky Mountains.

The century between 1820 and 1920 had given what we call civilization a chance to make many changes in the wild world of birds. During that time lifeless hummingbirds had been made to perch upon the hats of fashionable women; herring gulls had been robbed of their eggs and killed for their feathers; shooting movements had been organized to kill crows with shotgun or rifle, in order that more gunpowder might be sold; the people of Alaska had been permitted to kill more than eight thousand eagles in the last great breeding-place left to our National Emblem; uncounted millions of Passenger Pigeons had been slaughtered, and these wonderful birds done away with forever; and the methods by which egrets had been murdered were too horrible to write about in books for children to read.

But however shamefully civilization had treated, and had brought up children to treat, these and many other of their fellow creatures of the world, who had a right to the life that had been given them as surely as it had been given to men, the years since 1820 had been happy ones for the ancestors of Eve and Petro.

Eve and Petro, themselves, were happy as any two swallows need be that spring of 1920, when they started forth to seek a cliff, just as their ancestors had done for the hundred years or so since man began to notice their habits, and no man knows for how many hundreds of years before that.

Of course they found it as all cliff swallows must, for cliff-hunting is a part of their springtime work. It was very high and very straight. Its wall was of boards, and the gray shingled roof jutted out overhead just as if inviting Eve and Petro to its shelter.

It was a good cliff, and mankind had been so busy building the same sort all across the country for the past hundred years that there was no lack of them anywhere, and swallows could now choose the ones that pleased them best. Yes, civilization had been kind to them and had made more cliffs than Nature had built for them; though perhaps it was Mother Nature, herself, who taught the birds that these structures men called barns and used inside for hay or cattle were, after all, only cliffs outside, and that people were harmless creatures who would not hurt the swallow kind.

However all that may be, it is quite certain that Eve and Petro squeaked pleasantly for joy when they chose their building site, undisturbed by the ladder that was soon put near, and unafraid of the people who climbed up to watch them at their work. They were too happily busy to worry, and besides, there is a tradition that men folk and swallow folk are friendly, each to the other.

How old this tradition is, we do not know; but we do know that swallows of one kind and another were welcomed in the Old World in the old days to heathen temples before there were Christian churches, and that to-day in the New World they play in and out of the dark arches in the great churches of far Brazil and flash across the gilding of the very tabernacle, reminding us of the passage in the Psalms where it is written that the swallow hath found a nest for herself, where she may lay her young—even thine altars, O Lord of Hosts!

So it is not strange that far and wide over the world people have the idea that swallows bring luck to the house. I think so myself, don't you?—that it is very good fortune, indeed, to have these birds of friendly and confiding ways beneath our shelter.

Of course the ancestors of cliff swallows had not known the walls and roofs of man so long as other kinds of swallows; but the associations of one short century had been pleasant enough to call forth many cheerful squeakings of joy, just like those of Eve and Petro that pleasant day in June when they started their nest under the roof near the top of the ladder.

To be sure, they made no use of that ladder, even though they were masons and had their hods of plaster to carry way up near the top of their cliff. No, they needed no firmer ladder than the air, and their long wings were strong enough to climb it with.

They lost little time in beginning, each coming with his first hod of plaster. How? Balanced on their heads as some people carry burdens? No. On their backs, then? No. In their claws? Oh, no, their feet were far too feeble for bearing loads. Do you remember what Corbie used for a berry-pail when he went out to pick fruit? Why, of course! the hod of the swallow mason is none other than his mouth, and it holds as much as half a thimbleful.

First, Eve had to mark the place where the curved edge of the nest would be; and how could she mark it without any chalk, and how could she make a curve without any compasses? Well, she clung to the straight wall with her little feet, which she kept nearly in one place, and, swinging her body about, hitch by hitch, she struck out her curve with her beak and marked it with little dabs of plaster. Then she and Petro could tell where to build and, taking turns, first one and then the other, they began to lay the wall of their home.

It was slow work, for it must be thick and strong, and the place where they gathered the plaster was not handy by, and it took a great great many trips, their hods being so small.

At first, while the nest was shallow, only one could work at a time; and if Petro came back with his plaster before Eve had patted the last of hers into place, she would squeak at him in a fidgety though not fretful voice, as if saying, "Now, don't get in my way and bother me, dear." So he would have to fly about while he waited for her to go. The minute she was ready to be off, he would be slipping into her place; and this time she would give him a cosy little squeak of welcome, and he would reply, with his mouth full of plaster, in a quick and friendly way, as if he meant, "I'll build while you fetch more plaster, and we'd both better hurry, don't you think?"

After worrying a bit about the best place to dump his hodful, he went to work. He opened his beak and, in the most matter-of-fact way, pushed out his lump of plaster with his tongue, on top of the nest wall. Then he braced his body firmly in the nest and began to use his trowel, which was his upper beak, pushing the fresh lump all smooth on the inside of the nest.

Have you ever seen a dog poke with the top of his nose, until he got the dirt heaped over a bone which he had buried? Well, that's much the way Petro bunted his plaster smooth—rooted it into place with the top of his closed beak. He got his face dirty doing it, too, even the pretty pale feather crescent moon on his forehead. But that didn't matter. Trowels, if they do useful work, have to get dirty doing it, and Petro didn't stop because of that. If he had, his nest would have been as rough on the inside as it was outside, where a humpy little lump showed for each mouthful of plaster.

Although Eve and Petro did not fly off to the plaster pit together, they did not go alone, for there was a whole colony of swallows building under the eaves of that same barn; and while some of them stayed and plastered, the rest flew forth for a fresh supply.

They knew the place, every one of them; and swiftly over the meadow and over the marsh they flew, until they came to a pasture. There, near a spring where the cows had trampled the ground until it was oozy and the water stood in tiny pools in their hoof prints, the swallows stopped. They put down their beaks into the mud and gathered it in their mouths; and all the time they held their wings quivering up over their beautiful blue backs, like a flock of butterflies just alighting with their wings atremble.

So their plaster pit was just a mud-puddle. Yes, that is all; only it had to be a particularly sticky kind of mud, which is called clay; for the walls of their homes were a sort of brick something like that the people made in Egypt years and years ago. And do you remember how the story goes that the folk in Pharaoh's day gathered straws to mix with the clay, so that their bricks would be stronger? Well, Eve and Petro didn't know that story, but they gathered fibres of slender roots and dead grass stems with their clay, which doubtless did their brick plaster no harm.

At Work in the Plaster Pit.

Men brick-makers nowadays bake their bricks in ovens called kilns, which are heated with fire. Eve and Petro let their brick bake, too, and the fire they used was the same one the Egyptians used in the days of Pharaoh—a fire that had never in all that time gone out, but had glowed steadily century after century, baking many bricks for folk and birds. Of course you know what fire that is, for you see it yourself every day that the sun shines.

Every now and again Eve and Petro and all the rest of the swallow colony left off their brick-building and went on a hunting trip. They hunted high in the air and they hunted low over the meadow. They hunted afar off along the stream and they hunted near by in the barnyard. And all the game they caught they captured on the wing, and they ate it fresh at a gulp without pausing in their flight. As they sailed and swirled, they were good to watch, for a swallow's strong long wings bear him right gracefully.

Why did they stop for the hunting flight? Perhaps they were hungry. Perhaps their mouths were tired of being hods for clay they could not eat. Perhaps the fresh plaster on the walls of their homes needed time to dry a bit before more was added.

Be that as it may, they made the minutes count even while they rested from their building work. For they used this time getting their meals; and whenever they were doing that, they were working for the owner of the barn, paying their rent for the house-lot on the wall by catching grass insects over the meadow, and mosquitoes and horseflies and house-flies by the hundreds, and many another pest, too.

The Hunting Flight.

Ah, yes, there may be some reason for the belief that swallows bring good luck to men. I once heard of a farmer who said he didn't dare disturb these birds because of a superstition that, if he did, his cows wouldn't give so much milk. Well, maybe they wouldn't if all the flies a colony of swallows could catch were alive to pester his herd; for the happier and more comfortable these animals are, the healthier they are and the more milk they give.

The hunting flights of Eve and Petro and their comrades lasted about fifteen minutes each time they took a recess from their building.

After two days the nest was big enough, so that there was room for both swallows to build at once; and after that, Petro didn't have to fly around with his mouth full of plaster waiting for Eve to go if he chanced to come before she was through. They always chatted a bit and then went on with their work, placing their plaster carefully and bunting it smooth on the inside, modeling with clay a house as well suited to their needs as is the concrete mansion a human architect makes suited to the needs of man.

And if you think it is a simple matter to make a nest of clay, just go to the wisest architect you know and ask him these questions. How many hodfuls of clay, each holding as much as half a thimble, would it take to build the wall of a room just the right shape for a swallow to sit in while she brooded her eggs? How large would it have to be inside, to hold four or five young swallows grown big enough for their first flight? How thick would the walls have to be to make it strong enough? What sort of curve would be best for its support against a perfectly straight wall? How much space would have to be allowed for lining the room, to make it warm and comfortable? How can the clay be handled so that the drying sun and wind will not crack the walls? What is the test for telling whether the clay is sticky enough to hold together? How much of the nest must be stuck to the cliff so that the weight of it will not make it fall?

If the architect can answer all those questions, ask him one more: ask him if he could make such a nest with the same materials the birds used, and with no more tools?

Well, Eve and Petro could and did. It was big enough and strong enough and shaped just right; and when it was nearly done and nearly ready for the soft warm lining, That Boy climbed the ladder and knocked it down with his hand.

There it lay, Eve and Petro's wonderfully modeled nest of clay, broken to bits on the ground and spoiled, oh, quite spoiled. There is a saying that it brings bad luck to do harm to a swallow. What bad luck, then, had the hand of That Boy brought to the world that day?

They always chatted a bit and then went on with their work, placing their plaster carefully.

Bad luck it brought to Eve and Petro, who had toiled patiently and unafraid beside the ladder-top, with faith in those who climbed quietly to watch the little feathered masons at their work. But now the walls of their home were broken and crumbled, and their faith was broken and crumbled, too. In dismay they cried out when they saw what was happening, and in dismay their swallow comrades cried out with them. Fear and disappointment entered their quick hearts, which had been beating in confidence and hope. People who climbed ladders were not beings to trust, after all, but frightful and destroying creatures. This had the hand of That Boy brought to Eve and Petro, who looked at the empty place where their nest had been, and went away.

Bad luck it brought to an artist who drew pictures of birds; and when he knew what had happened, a sudden light flamed in his eyes. The name of this light is anger—the kind that comes when harm has been ruthlessly done to the weak and helpless. For the artist had climbed the ladder many a time, and had laid his quiet hand upon the lower curve of the nest while Eve and Petro went on with their building at the upper edge. And he had seen the colors of their feathers and the shape of the pale crescent on their foreheads—the mark a man named Say had noticed many years before, when he named this swallow in Latin, *lunifrons*, because *luna* means moon and *frons* means front. And he had hoped to climb the ladder many a time again, and when there should be young in the nest, to see how they looked and watch what they did, so that he could draw pictures of the children of Eve and Petro.

Bad luck it brought to a writer of bird stories; and when she knew what had happened, something like an ache in her throat seemed to choke her, something that is called anger—the kind that comes when harm is done to little folk we love. For she had climbed the ladder many a time, and had rested her head against the top while she watched Eve and Petro push the pellets of mud from their mouths with their tongues and bunt the wall of their clay nest smooth on the inside with the top of their closed beaks, not stopping even though they brushed their pretty chestnut-colored cheeks against the sticky mud, or got specks on the feathers of their dainty foreheads that bore a mark shaped like a pale new moon. And she had hoped to climb the ladder many a time again, and watch Eve and Petro feed their children when the nest was done and lined and the eggs were laid and hatched; for this nest could be looked into, as the top was left open because the barn roof sheltered it and it needed no other cover.

Now Eve and Petro were gone, and no more sketches could be made near enough to show how little cliff swallows looked in their nest. And nothing more could be written about such affairs of these two birds as could only be learned close to them. Nor, indeed, was there any way to learn those things from the rest of the colony; for it so chanced that Eve and Petro were the only pair who had built where a ladder could be placed. So bad luck had come not only to Eve and Petro, but to the story of their lives.

But, most of all, the breaking of their nest brought bad luck to That Boy, himself. For as he stood at the top of the ladder, he might have curved the hollow of his hand gently upon the rounded outside of the nest and, waiting quietly, have watched the building birds. He might have seen Eve come flitting home with her tiny load of clay, poking it out of her mouth with her tongue and bunting it smooth in her own cunning way. He might have laid his head against the ladder and heard their cosy voices as they squeaked pleasantly together over the home-building. He might have looked at the colors of their feathers, and seen where they were glossy black with a greenish sheen, where rich purply chestnut, and where grayish white. He might have looked well at the pale feather moon on their foreheads, which the man named Say had noticed one hundred years before. He might, oh, he might have become one of the brotherhood of men, whom swallows of one kind or another have trusted since the far-off years of Bible times when they built at the altars of the Lord of Hosts.

All this good luck he held, That Boy, in the hollow of his hand, and he threw it away when he struck the nest; and it fell, crumbled, with the broken bits of clay.

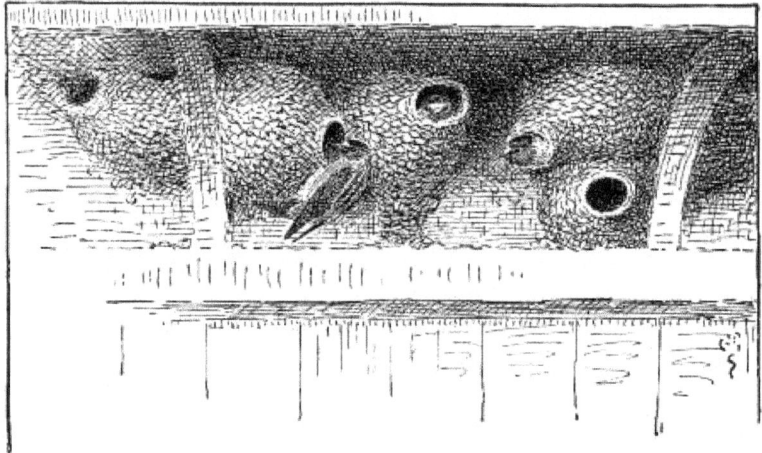

Quaint Clay Pottery.

As for Eve and Petro, if fear and disappointment had driven trust from their hearts, they still had courage and patience and industry. They sought another and a different sort of cliff, and found one made of red brick and white stone. Near the very high top of this a large colony of swallows were building; and, because there was no closely protecting roof, these swallows were making the round part of their nest closed over at the top with a winding hallway to an outer doorway. They looked, indeed, like a row of quaint clay pottery, shaped like crook-necked gourds. For such were the nests these swallows built one hundred years ago on the wild rock cliffs, if they chose their house-lots where there was no overhanging shelter; and such are the nests they still build when there seems to be need of them.

They were too far from the pleasant pasture to dig their clay out of the footprints of cows; but there was a track where the automobiles slushed through sticky mud, and they swirled down there and filled their little hods when the road was clear.

Eve and Petro found a nook even higher up than the others, where a crook-necked jug of a nest did not seem to fit. When they had built their wall as high as need be, they closed it over with a little rounded dome, and at the side they left two doorways open, one facing the southwest and one facing the southeast. And some days after this was done, had you gone to the foot of their cliff and used a pair of field-glasses, you might have seen Eve's head sticking out of one door and Petro's at the other. Ah, they had, then, some good luck left them. They had had each other in their days of trouble, and now they rested from their building labors and sat happily together in their second home, each with a doorway to enjoy.

And later on they had more good luck still. For there came a day when they spent no more time sitting at ease within doors, but flew hither and yon, and then, returning to the nest, clung outside with their tiny feet and stuck their heads in at the open doorway for a brief moment before they were off again. Their nest was too far up for anyone to hear or see what went on within; but there must have been some hungry little mouths yawning all day long, to keep Eve and Petro both so busy hunting the air for insects.

Soon after this one of the doors was closed, sealed tight with clay. What had happened? Were the little ones inside crowding about too recklessly, so that there was danger of one falling out? Had Eve and Petro come upon an especially good mud-puddle and built a bit more just for the fun of it?

It was not very many days after this that Eve and Petro and all their comrades ceased coming to the cliff where their curious nests were fastened. Their doorways knew them no more; but over the meadows from dawn till nearly dusk there flew beautiful old swallows bearing upon their foreheads the pale mark of a new moon, and with them were their young.

At night they sought the marshes, where their little feet might cling to slender stems of bending reeds; and their numbers were very many.

But winter would be coming, and if it still was a long way off, so were the hunting grounds of South America, where they must be flitting away the days when the northern marshes would be frozen over.

So off they went, Eve and Petro and their young, looking so much like others of the swallow flock that we could not tell who they were, now that they had stopped coming to their nest with one open and one closed doorway.

They would have far to travel, even if they took the direct over-water route, which many sorts of birds do. But what is distance to Petro, whose strong wings carry him lightly? A mile or a hundred or a thousand even are nothing if the hunting be good. Might just as well be flying south, as back and forth over the same meadow the livelong day, with now and then a rest on the roadside wires, which fit his little feet nearly as well as the reeds of the marsh.

Some people think it is for the sake of the hunting that the route of the swallows lies overland, for they fly by day and catch their game all along the way.

And as they journeyed, Eve and Petro and their flock, south and south and south, maybe the children, here and there, waved their hands to them and called, "Good hunting, little friends of the air, and *good luck* through all the winter till you come back to us again."

A Famous Landmark.

VI
UNCLE SAM

Uncle Sam stood at the threshold of his home, with an air of dignity. There was enough to fill his breast with honest pride. His home had been a famous landmark for generations before he himself had fallen heir to it. It was the oldest one in the neighborhood. It had stood there seventy-five years before, when a white man had built a cabin within sight of it, for company. That cabin had been neglected and had fallen to bits years ago; but Uncle Sam's ancestors had taken care of their place, and had mended the weak spots each season, and had kept it in such repair that it was still as good as ever. It would last, indeed, with such treatment, as long as the post and the beams that supported it held. The post was the trunk of a tall old tree, and the beams were the branches, so near the top that it would be a very brave or a very foolish man who would try to climb so far; for there were no stairs.

No stairs, and such a distance up! But Uncle Sam could find the path that led to it; for was he not a lord of the air, and could he not sail the roughest wind with those strong wings of his?

Above all other creatures of this great land he had been honored.

Perhaps it was the sure strength of his wings that gave him a stately poise of pride even as he rested. It could not have been the honor men had bestowed upon him; for, although that was very great, he knew nothing about it.

Soldiers had gone into battle for freedom and right, bearing the picture of Uncle Sam on their banners. Veterans had walked in Memorial Day parades, while over their gray heads floated the symbol of Uncle Sam and the Stars and Stripes. Yes, the people of a great and noble land, reaching from a sea on the east to a sea on the west, had honored Uncle Sam by choosing him for the emblem of their country. His picture was stamped on their paper money, and ornamented one side of the coins that came from the mint, with the words, "In God We Trust," on the other side. Above all other creatures of this great land he had been honored; and could he have understood, he might well have been justly proud of this tribute.

But as it was, perhaps his emotions were centred only on his family; for his home was shared by his mate and two young sons. He bent his white head to look down at his twins. They were such hungry rascals and needed such a deal of care! They had needed care, indeed, ever since the day their little bodies had begun to form in the two bluish white eggs their mother had laid in the nest. They had stayed inside those shells for a month; and they never could have lived and grown there if they had not been brooded and kept warm. Their mother had snuggled her feathers over them and kept them cosy; and, when she had needed a change and a rest, Uncle Sam had cuddled them close under his body; for a month is a long time to keep eggs from getting cold, and it was only fair that he should take his turn.

He was no shirk in his family life. He had chosen his mate until death should part them; and whenever there were eggs in the nest, he was as patient about brooding them as she was; for did they not belong to both of them, and did they not contain two fine young eagles in the making?

And never had they had finer children than the two who that moment were opening hungry mouths and begging for food. In answer to their teasing, Uncle Sam spread his great wings and took stately flight to the lake. For he was a fisherman. When a fish came to the surface, he would try to catch it in his strong claws, so that he might have food to take back to his waiting family. This was easy for him when the fish was wounded or weak and had come to the surface to die; but the quick fishes often escaped, because he was not so skillful at this sort of fishing as the osprey.

Yes, the osprey was a wonderful fisherman, who could snatch a fish from the water in his sure claws. But for all that, he was not so wonderful as Uncle Sam, who could catch a fish in the air.

The Yankee-Doodle Twins.

Now, fishing in the air was a thrilling game that Uncle Sam loved. All the wild delight of a chase was in the sport. He used, sometimes, to sit high up on a cliff and watch the osprey swoop down to the water. Then, when the hawk mounted with the prize, Uncle Sam flew far above him and swept downward, commanding him to drop the fish. The smaller bird obeyed, and let the fish fall from his claws. But it never fell far. Uncle Sam closed his mighty wings and dropped with such speed that he caught the fish in mid-air; and the tree-tops swayed with the sudden wind his passing caused. Surely there was never a more exciting way of going fishing than this!

And did the fish belong to the osprey or to Uncle Sam?

What would you call a man who, by power of greater strength, took away the food another man had earned?

Are we, then, to call Uncle Sam a thief and a bully?

Ah, no; because it is not with an eagle as it is with a man.

For the wild things of the world there is only one law, and that is the Law of Nature. They must live as they are made to live, and that is all that concerns them. There is nothing for bird or beast or blossom to learn about "right" or "wrong," as we learn about those things. All they need to do—any of them—is to live naturally.

When we think about it that way, it is very easy to tell whether the fish belonged to the osprey or to Uncle Sam. Of course, to begin with, the fish belonged to itself as long as it could dive quickly enough or swim fast enough to keep itself free and safe. But the minute the osprey caught it, it belonged to the osprey, just as much as it would belong to you if you caught it with a net or a hook. Yes, the fish belonged to the osprey *more* than it would belong to you; for ospreys hunted food for themselves and for their young in that lake centuries and centuries before a white man even saw it, and before nets and hooks were invented; and besides, in most places, the children of men can live and grow if they never eat a fish, while the children of the osprey would die without such food. So we admire Fisherman Osprey for his strength and swiftness and skill, and are glad for him when he flies off with the prize, which is his very own as long as he can keep it.

But when he drops it, it is his no longer, but the eagle's, who fishes wonderfully in the air—a game depending on the keenness of his sight, his strength, his quickness, and his skill; and the fish that belonged first to itself, and then to the osprey, belonged in the end to the eagle; and all this is according to the Law of Nature.

Uncle Sam was not selfish about that fish. He gave it to his twins, and they did enjoy their dinner very, very much, indeed. A fresh brook trout, browned just right, never tasted better to you. For they had been hungry, and the food was good for them.

Uncle Sam and his mate, whom the children who lived within sight of their nest named Aunt Samantha, had many a hunting and fishing trip to take while the twins were growing; for the bigger the young eagles became, the bigger their appetites were, too. But at last the youngsters were old enough and strong enough and brave enough to take their first flight. Think of them, then, standing there on the outer porch of their great home in the air, and daring to leave it, when it was so very high and they would have so very far to fall if their wings did not work right!

Nonsense, an eagle fall! Had they not been stretching and exercising their muscles for days? And surely the twins would succeed, with Uncle Sam and Aunt Samantha to encourage and urge them forth.

The day Uncle Sam cheered his young sons in their baby flight was a great day for all the country round. For not only were the sons of eagles flying, but the sons of men were flying, too. Yes, it was practice day near the lake, and across the water airships rose from the camp and sailed through the air, like mighty birds meant for mighty deeds. For Uncle Sam's country was at war, and many brave and noble lads thrilled with pride because they were going to help win a battle for Right.

The bravest and noblest and most fearless of all the camp caught sight of Uncle Sam and smiled. "Emblem of my country!" the young man said. "King of the air in your strong flight! Great deeds are to be done, O Eagle with the snow-white head, and your banner will be foremost in the fight."

Uncle Sam made no reply. He was too far away to hear, and he could not have understood if he had been near. He saw the distant airships, so big and strong, and led his family away to quieter places, without knowing at all what the big birds were, or what they meant to do. There was so much happening in the country that honored him, that Uncle Sam could not understand!

He did not even know that, far to the northwest, there was a part of the country called Alaska, where eagles had lived in safety and had brought up their young in peace long after their haunts in most parts of the land had been disturbed. He did not know that the government of Alaska was at that moment paying people fifty cents for every eagle they would kill, and that in two years about five thousand of these noble birds were to die in that manner. He did not know that, if such deeds kept on, before many years there would be no eagles flying proudly through the air: there would be only pictures of eagles on our money and banners. If he could have been told what was happening, and that there was danger that the country would be without a living emblem, and that there might be only stuffed emblems in museums, would he not have thought, "Surely the strong, wise men who go forth to fight for right and liberty will see that the bird of freedom has a home in their land!"

No; Uncle Sam knew nothing about such matters, and so he busied his mind with the things he did know, and was not sad.

He knew where the swamp was, and in the swamp the ducks were thick. They were good-tasting ducks, and there were so many of them that hunters with guns and dogs gathered there from all the country round. And the hunters wounded some birds that the dogs did not get, and these could not fly off at migrating time.

Now, Uncle Sam and his family found the wounded ducks easy to catch, and they were nearly as well pleased with them for food as with fish. Of course their feathers had to be picked off first. No eagle would eat a duck with his feathers on, any more than you would. And Uncle Sam knew how to strip off the feathers as well as anyone.

So it was interesting in the swamp, and Uncle Sam and Aunt Samantha and the twins were satisfied with hunting there when they were not fishing in the lake.

One day, when Uncle Sam went hunting, he flew near a field where there was a little lamb; and being a strong and powerful eagle, he was able to carry it away. Perhaps he felt very proud as he flew off with so much food at one time. Such strength is something to be pleased with when it is put to the right use, and getting food is as important for an eagle's life as it is for a man's.

He lifted his burden high in the air, holding it in his strong talons; and he did not falter once in his steady flight, although the load weighed nearly as much as he did, and he carried it two miles without resting once.

Yes, I think Uncle Sam was proud of that day's hunting and happy with what he had caught; and the tender meat tasted good to him and his family.

But the man who had owned the lamb before Uncle Sam caught it was not pleased. He happened to be coming out of the woods just in time to see the capture; and an hour later the boy and the girl who lived within sight of Uncle Sam's nest met the man and saw that he carried a gun.

"I'm after a white-headed sheep thief," he said; "do you know which way he flew, after he reached the cliff?"

The boy's face turned white in a second, and he held his fists together very still and very tight. The girl looked at her younger brother and then at the man.

"Yes, we know," she said, "and we will not tell."

"Why?" asked the man. "He took the lamb I was going to roast when it was big enough."

The girl chuckled a little merrily. "And Uncle Sam got ahead of you," she said. "Never mind, I'll get the money to pay for his dinner. The eagles here usually eat fish from the lake, and sometimes game from the swamp; but once in a very, very long while they take a lamb. When that happens, the Junior Audubon Society at our school pays for their treat. I have the money, because I am treasurer."

After the girl turned back to the house for the money, the boy looked hard at the gun. Then he swallowed to get rid of the lump that hurt his throat and said, "If you had shot Uncle Sam or Aunt Samantha or their young, the children for miles and miles NEVER would have liked you. Eagles have nested in that tree for more than seventy years, and nobody except a newcomer would think of shooting one."

So they talked together for some time about eagles; and when the girl came back, the man did not charge so much for Uncle Sam's treat as we sometimes have to pay for our own lamb chops.

And way off among the cliffs Uncle Sam ate in content, not knowing that his life had been in danger, and that he had been saved by a boy and a girl who were growing up "under the shadow of an eagle's wings," as they said to each other as they watched him sail the air in his journeys to and fro.

That afternoon, when they heard him call, "Cac, cac, cac," they said, "Uncle Sam is laughing." And when his mate answered in her harsh voice, they said, "Aunt Samantha would be happy if she knew we saved their lives."

Busy with the life Nature taught them to live, the twins grew up as Uncle Sam had grown before them.

As they were hunters, there was nothing more interesting to them than seeking their food in wild, free places. They had no guns and dogs, but they caught game in the swamp. They had no cooks to prepare their ducks, so they picked off the feathers themselves. They had no fish-line and tackle, but they caught fish in the lake. And in time they caught fish in the air, too; which was even more thrilling, and a game they came to enjoy when they overtook the ospreys. Many times, too, they sought the fish that had been washed up on the lake shore, and so helped keep things sweet and clean. In this way they were scavengers; and it is always well to remember that a scavenger, whether he be a bird or beast or beetle, does great service in the world for all who need pure air to breathe.

The first year they became bigger than their father, and bigger than they themselves would be when they were old. At first, too, their eyes were brown, and not yellow like their father's and mother's. And for two years their heads and tails were dark, so that they looked much more like "golden eagles" than they did like the old ones of their own kind.

The soldiers at the training-camp caught sight of them now and then, and named them the "Yankee-Doodle Twins." When the twins were three years old, their molting season brought a remarkable change to them. The dark feathers of their heads and necks and tails dropped out, and in their places white feathers grew, so that by this time they looked like their own father and mother, who are what is called "bald eagles," though their heads are not bald at all, but well covered with feathers.

These two birds that were hatched in the home that was more than seventy years old lived to see the end of the war the young soldiers were training for when they took their first flights together near the shore of the same lake. And perhaps they will live to a time when the people of their country learn to deal more and more justly with each other and with the great bird of freedom chosen by their forefathers to be the emblem of their proud land.

Why, indeed, if the boys and girls of the neighborhood keep up a guard for the protection of Uncle Sam and Aunt Samantha, should they not nest again, and yet again, in that tree-top home that has been so well taken care of for more than threescore years and ten; and bring up Yankee-Doodle Twins for their country in days of peace as they did in days of war?

VII
CORBIE

Corbie's great-great-grandfather ruled a large flock from his look-out throne on a tall pine stump, where he could see far and wide, and judge for his people where they should feed and when they should fly.

His great-grandfather was famous for his collections of old china and other rare treasures, having lived in the woods near the town dump, where he picked up many a bright trinket, chief among which was an old gold-plated watch-chain, which he kept hidden in a doll's red tea-cup when he was not using it.

His grandfather was a handsome fellow, so glistening that he looked rather purple when he walked in the sunshine; and he had a voice so sweet and mellow that any minstrel might have been proud of it, though he seldom sang, and it is possible that no one but Corbie's grandmother heard it at its best. He was, moreover, a merry soul, fond of a joke, and always ready to dance a jig, with a chuckle, when anything very funny happened in crowdom.

As for the wisdom and beauty of his grandmothers all the way back, there is so much to be said that, if I once began to tell about them, there would be no space left for the story of Corbie himself.

In this Mother Crow had laid her eggs.

Of course, coming from a family like that, Corbie was sure to be remarkable; for there is no doubt at all that we inherit many traits of our ancestors.

Corbie knew very little about his own father and mother, for he was adopted into a human family when he was ten days old, and a baby at that age does not remember much.

Although he was too young to realize it, those first ten days after he had come out of his shell, and those before that, while he was growing inside his shell, were in some ways the most important of his life, for it was then that he needed the most tender and skillful care. Well, he had it; for the gentleness and skill of Father and Mother Crow left nothing to be desired. They had built the best possible nest for their needs by placing strong sticks criss-cross high up in an old pine tree. For a lining they had stripped soft stringy bark from a wild grapevine, and had finished off with a bit of still softer dried grass.

In this Mother Crow had laid her five bluish-green eggs marked with brown; and she and Father Crow had shared, turn and turn about, the long task of keeping their babies inside those beautiful shells warm enough so that they could grow.

And grow they did, into five as homely little objects as ever broke their way out of good-looking eggshells. There was not down on their bodies to make them fluffy and pretty, like Peter Piper's children. They were just sprawling little bits of crow-life, so helpless that it would have been quite pitiful if they had not had a good patient mother and a father who seemed never to get tired of hunting for food.

Now, it takes a very great deal of food for five young crows, because each one on some days will eat more than half his own weight and beg for more. Dear, dear! how they did beg! Every time either Father or Mother Crow came back to the nest, those five beaks would open so wide that the babies seemed to be yawning way down to the end of their red throats. Oh, the food that got stuffed into them! Good and nourishing, every bit of it; for a proper diet is as important to a bird baby as to a human one. Juicy caterpillars—a lot of them: enough to eat up a whole berry-patch if the crows hadn't found them; nutty-flavored grasshoppers—a lot of them, too; so many, in fact, that it looked very much as if crows were the reason the grasshoppers were so nearly wiped out that year that they didn't have a chance to trouble the farmers' crops; and now and then a dainty egg was served them in the most tempting crow-fashion, that is, right from the beak of the parent.

For, as you no doubt have heard, a crow thinks no more of helping himself to an egg of a wild bird than we do of visiting the nests of tame birds, such as hens and geese and turkeys, and taking the eggs they lay. Of course, it would not occur to a crow that he didn't have a perfect right to take such food for himself and his young as he could find in his day's hunting. Indeed, it is not unlikely that, if a crow did any real thinking about the matter, he might decide that robins and meadowlarks were his chickens anyway. So what the other birds would better do about it is to hide their nests as well as ever they can, and be quiet when they come and go.

That is the way Father and Mother Crow did, themselves, when they built their home where the pine boughs hid it from climbers below and from fliers above. And, though you might hardly believe it of a crow, they were still as mice whenever they came near it, alighting first on trees close by, and slipping up carefully between the branches, to be sure no enemy was following their movements. Then they would greet their babies with a comforting low

"Caw," which seemed to mean, "Never fear, little ones, we've brought you a very good treat." Yes, they were shy, those old crows, when they were near their home, and very quiet they kept their affairs until their young got into the habit of yelling, "Kah, kah, kah," at the top of their voices whenever they were hungry, and of mumbling loudly, "Gubble-gubble-gubble," whenever they were eating.

After that time comes, there is very little quiet within the home of a crow; and all the world about may guess, without being a bit clever, where the nest is. A good thing it is for the noisy youngsters that by that time they are so large that it does not matter quite so much.

But it was before the "kah-and-gubble" habit had much more than begun that Corbie was adopted; and the nestlings were really as still as could be when the father of the Brown-eyed Boy and the Blue-eyed Girl climbed way, way, way up that big tree and looked into the round little room up there. There was no furniture—none at all. Just one bare nursery, in which five babies were staying day and night. Yet it was a tidy room, fresh and sweet enough for anybody to live in; for a crow, young or old, is a clean sort of person.

The father of the Brown-eyed Boy and the Blue-eyed Girl looked over the five homely, floundering little birds, and, choosing Corbie, put him into his hat and climbed down with him. He was a nimble sort of father, or he never could have done it, so tall a tree it was, with no branches near the ground.

Corbie, even at ten days old, was not like the spry children of Peter Piper, who could run about at one day old, all ready for picnics and teetering along the shore. No, indeed! He was almost as helpless and quite as floppy as a human baby, and he needed as good care, too. He needed warmth enough and food enough and a clean nest to live in; and he needed to be kept safe from such prowling animals as will eat young birds, and from other enemies. All these things his father and mother had looked out for.

Now the little Corbie was kidnaped—taken away from his home and the loving and patient care of his parents.

But you need not be sorry for Corbie—not very. For the Brown-eyed Boy and the Blue-eyed Girl adopted the little chap, and gave him food enough and warmth enough and a chance to keep his new nest clean; and they did it all with love and patience, too.

Corbie kept them busy, for they were quick to learn that, when he opened his beak and said, "Kah," it was meal-time, even if he had had luncheon only ten minutes before. His throat was very red and very hollow, and seemed ready to swallow no end of fresh raw egg and bits of raw beef and earthworms and bread soaked in milk. Not that he had to have much at a time, but he needed so very many meals a day. It was fun to feed the little fellow, because he grew so fast and because he was so comical when he called, "Kah."

It was not long before his body looked as if he had a crop of paint-brushes growing all over it; for a feather, when it first comes, is protected by a little case, and the end of the feather, which sticks out of the tip of the case, does look very much like the soft hairs at the end of a paint-brush, the kind that has a hollow quill stem, you know. After they were once started, dear me, how those feathers grew! It seemed no time at all before they covered up the ear-holes in the side of his head, and no time at all before a little bristle fringe grew down over the nose-holes in his long horny beak.

He was nearly twenty days old before he could stand up on his toes like a grown-up crow. Before that, when he stood up in his nest and "kahed" for food, he stood on his whole foot way back to the heel, which looks like a knee, only it bends the wrong way. When he was about three weeks old, however, he began standing way up on his toes, and stretching his leg till his heels came up straight. Then he would flap his wings and exercise them, too.

Of course, you can guess what that meant. It meant—yes, it meant that Corbie was getting ready to leave his nest; and before the Brown-eyed Boy and the Blue-eyed Girl really knew what was happening, Corbie went for his first ramble. He stepped out of his nest-box, which had been placed on top of a flat, low shed, and strolled up the steep roof of the woodshed, which was within reach. There he stood on the ridge-pole, the little tike, and yelled, "Caw," in almost a grown-up way, as if he felt proud and happy. Perhaps he did for a while. It really was a trip to be proud of for one's very first walk in the world.

But the exercise made him hungry, and he soon yelled, "Kah!" in a tone that meant, "Bring me my luncheon this minute or I'll beg till you do."

The Brown-eyed Boy took a dish of bread and milk to the edge of the low roof, where the nest-box had been placed, and the Blue-eyed Girl called, "Come and get it, Corbie."

Not Corbie! He had always had his meals brought to him. He liked service, that crow. And besides, maybe he *couldn't* walk down the roof it had been so easy to run up. Anyway, his voice began to sound as if he were scared as well as hungry, and later as if he were more scared than hungry.

Now it stood to reason that Corbie's meals could not be served him every fifteen minutes on the ridge-pole of a steep roof. So the long ladder had to be brought out, and the crow carried to the ground and advised to keep within easy reach until he could use his wings.

It was only a few days until Corbie could fly down from anything he could climb up; and from that hour he never lacked for amusement. Of course, the greedy little month-old baby found most of his fun for a while in being fed. "Kah! Kah! Kah!" he called from sun-up to sun-down, keeping the Brown-eyed Boy and the Blue-eyed Girl busy digging earthworms and cutworms and white grubs, and soaking bread in milk for him. "Gubble-gubble-gubble," he said as he swallowed it—it was all so very good.

"Kah! Kah! Kah!" he called from sun-up to sun-down.

The joke of it was that Corbie, even then, had a secret—his first one. He had many later on. But the very first one seems the most wonderful, somehow. Yes, he could feed himself long before he let his foster brother and sister know it; and I think, had he been a wild crow instead of a tame one, he would have fooled his own father and mother the same way—the little rascal.

No one would think, to see him with beak up and open, and with fluttering wings held out from his sides, that the little chap begging "Kah! kah! kah!" was old enough to do more than "gubble" the food that was poked into his big throat. But for all that, when the Brown-eyed Boy forgot the dish of earthworms and ran off to play, Corbie would listen until he could hear no one near, and then cock his bright eye down over the wriggling worms. Then, very slyly, he would pick one up with a jerk and catch it back into his mouth. One by one he would eat the worms, until he wanted no more; and then he would hide the rest by poking them into cracks or covering them with chips, crooning the while over his secret joke. "There-there-tuck-it-there," was what his croon sounded like; but if the Brown-eyed Boy or the Blue-eyed Girl came near, he would flutter out his wings at his sides and lift his open beak, his teasing "Kah" seeming to say, "Honest, I haven't had a bite to eat since you fed me last."

When his body was grown so big with his stuffing that he was almost a full-sized crow, he stopped his constant begging for food. The days of his greed were only the days of his growth needs, and the world was too full of adventures to spend all his time just eating.

It was now time for him to take pleasure in his sense of sight, and for a few, weeks he went nearly crazy with joy over yellow playthings. He strewed the vegetable garden with torn and tattered squash-blossoms—gorgeous bits of color that it was such fun to find hidden under the big green leaves! He strutted to the flower-garden, and pulled off all the yellow pansies, piling them in a heap. He jumped for the golden buttercups, nipping them from their stems. He danced for joy among the torn dandelion blooms he threw about the lawn. For Corbie was like a human baby in many ways. He must handle what he loved, and spoil it with his playing.

Perhaps Corbie inherited his dancing from his grandfather. It may have come down to him with that old crow's merry spirit. Whether it was all his own or in part his grandfather's, it was a wonderful dance, so full of joy that the Brown-eyed Boy and the Blue-eyed Girl would leave their play to watch him, and would call the Grown-Ups of the household, that they, too, might see Corbie's "Happy Dance."

If he was pleased with his cleverness in hiding some pretty beetle in a crack and covering it with a chip, he danced. If he spied the shiny nails in the tool-shed, he danced. If he found a gay ribbon to drag about the yard, he danced. But most and best he danced on a hot day when he was given a bright basin of water. Singing a lively chattering tune, he came to his bath. He cocked one bright eye and then the other over the ripples his beak made in the water. Plunging in, he splashed long, cooling flutters. Then he danced back and forth from the doorstep to his glistening pan, chattering his funny tune the while.

Have you heard of a Highland Fling or a Sailor's Hornpipe? Well, Corbie's Happy Dance was as gay as both together, when he jigged in the dooryard to the tune of his own merry chatter. The Brown-eyed Boy and the Blue-eyed Girl laughed to see him, and the Grown-Ups laughed. And even as they laughed, their hearts danced with the little black crow—he made them feel so very glad about the bath. For he had been too warm and was now comfortable. The summer sun on his feathered body had tired him, and the cooling water brought relief. "Thanks be for the bath. O bird, be joyful for the bath!" he chattered in his own language, as he spread his wings and gave again and yet again his Happy Dance.

But a basin, however bright, is not enough to keep a crow in the dooryard; for a crow is a bird of adventure.

So it was that on a certain day Corbie flew over the cornfield and over the tree-tops to the river; and so quiet were his wings, that the Brown-eyed Boy and the Blue-eyed Girl did not hear his coming, and they both jumped when he perched upon a tiny rock near by and screamed, "Caw," quite suddenly, as one child says, "Boo," to another, to surprise him. Then the bird sang his chatter tune, and found a shallow place near the bank, where he splashed and bathed. After that, the Blue-eyed Girl showed him a little water-snail. He turned it over in his beak and dropped it. It meant no more to him than a pebble. "I think you'll like to eat it, Corbie," said the Brown-eyed Boy, breaking the shell and giving it to him again; "even people eat snails, I've heard."

Corbie took the morsel and swallowed it, and soon was cracking for himself all the snails his comrades gave him. But that was not enough, for their eyes were only the eyes of children and his bright bird eyes could find them twice as fast. So he waded in the river, playing "I spy" with his foster brother and sister, and beating them, too, at the game, though they had hunted snails as many summers as he had minutes.

He enjoyed doing many of the same things the children did. It was that, and his sociable, merry ways, that made him such a good playfellow, and because he wanted them to be happy in his pleasure and to praise his clever tricks. Like other children, eating when he was hungry gave him joy, and at times he made a game of it that was fun for them all. Every now and then he would go off quietly by himself, and fill the hollow of his throat with berries from the bushes near the river-bank and, flying back to his friends, would spill out his fruit, uncrushed, in a little pile beside them while he crooned and chuckled about it. He seemed to have the same sort of good time picking berries in his throat cup and showing how many he had found that the children did in seeing which could first fill a tin cup before they sat down on the rocks to eat them.

One day the Brown-eyed Boy and the Blue-eyed Girl were down by the river, hunting for pearls. A pearl-hunter had shown them how to open freshwater clamshells without killing the clams. Suddenly Corbie walked up and, taking one of these hard-shelled animals right out of their hands, he flew high overhead and dropped it down on the rocks near by. Of course that broke the shell and of course Corbie came down and ate the clam, without needing any vinegar or butter on it to make it taste good to him. How he learned to do this, the children never knew. Perhaps he found out by just happening to drop one he was carrying, or perhaps he saw the wild crows drop their clams to break the shells: for after nesting season they used often to come down from the mountainside to fish by the river for snails and clams and crayfish, when they were not helping the farmers by eating up insects in the fields.

Corbie liked the crayfish, too, as well as people like lobsters and crabs, and he had many an exciting hunt, poking under the stones for them and pulling them out with his strong beak.

There seemed to be no end of things Corbie could do with that beak of his. Sometimes it was a little crowbar for lifting stones or bits of wood when he wanted to see what was underneath; for as every outdoor child, either crow or human, knows, very, very interesting things live in such places. Sometimes it was a spade for digging in the dirt. Sometimes it was a pick for loosening up old wood in the hollow tree where he kept his best treasures. Sometimes it worked like a nut-cracker, sometimes like a pair of forceps, and sometimes—oh, you can think of a dozen tools that beak of Corbie's was like. He was as well off as if he had a whole carpenter's chest with him all the time. But mostly it served like a child's thumb and forefinger, to pick berries, or to untie the bright hair-ribbons of the Blue-eyed Girl or the shoe-laces of the Brown-eyed Boy. And once in a long, long while, when some stupid child or Grown-Up, who did not know how to be civil to a crow, used him roughly, his beak became a weapon with which to pinch and to strike until his enemy was black and blue. For Corbie learned, as every sturdy person must, in some way or other, how to protect himself when there was need.

Yes, Corbie's beak was wonderful. Of course, lips are better on people in many ways than beaks would be; but we cannot do one tenth so many things with our mouths as Corbie could with his. To be sure, we do not need to, for we have hands to help us out. If our arms had grown into wings, though, as a bird's arms do, how should we ever get along in this world?

Corbie slipped off and amused himself.

The weeks passed by. A happy time for Corbie, whether he played with the children or slipped off and amused himself, as he had a way of doing now and then, after he grew old enough to feel independent. The world for him was full of adventure and joy. He never once asked, "What can I do now to amuse me?" Never once. His brain was so active that he could fill every place and every hour full to the brim of interest. He had a merry way about him, and a gay chatter that seemed to mean, "Oh, life to a crow is joy! JOY!" And because of all this, it was not only the Brown-eyed Boy and the Blue-eyed Girl who loved him. He won the hearts of even the Grown-Ups, who had sometimes found it hard to be patient with him during the first noisy days, when he tired them with his frequent baby "kah-and-gubble," before he could feed himself.

But, however bold and dashing he was during the day, whatever the sunny hours had held of mirth and dancing, whichever path he had trod or flown, whomever he had chummed with—when it was the time of dusk, little Corbie sought the one he loved best of all, the one who had been most gentle with him, and snuggling close to the side of the Blue-eyed Girl, tucked his head into her sleeve or under the hem of her skirt, and crooned his sleepy song which seemed to mean:—

Oh! soft and warm the crow in the nest
Finds the fluff of his mother's breast.
Oh! well he sleeps, for she folds him tight—
Safe from the owl that flies by night.

Oh! far her wings have fluttered away,
Nor does it matter in the day.
But keep me, pray, till again 't is light,
Safe from the owl that flies by night.

Thus, long after he would have been weaned, for his own good, from such care, had he remained wild, Corbie, the tame crow, claimed protection with cunning, cuddling ways that taught the Blue-eyed Girl and her brother and the Grown-Ups, too, something about crows that many people never even guess. For all their rollicking care-free ways, there is, hidden beneath their black feathers, an affection very tender and lasting; and when they are given the friendship of humans, they find touching ways of showing how deep their trust can be.

Before the summer was over, Corbie had as famous a collection as his great grandfather. The children knew where he kept it, and used sometimes to climb up to look at his playthings. They never disturbed them except to take out the knitting-needle, thimble, spoons, or things like that, which were needed in the house. The bright penny someone had given him, the shiny nails, the brass-headed tacks, the big white feather, the yellow marble, all the bits of colored glass, and an old watch, they left where he put them; for they thought that he loved his things, or he would not have hidden them together; and they thought, and so do I, that he had as much right to his treasures to look at and care for as the Brown-eyed Boy had to his collection of pretty stones and the Blue-eyed Girl to the flowers in her wild garden.

After his feathers were grown, in the spring, Corbie had been really good-looking in his black suit; but by the first of September he was homely again. His little side-feather moustache dropped out at the top of his beak, so that his nostrils were uncovered as they had been when he was very young. The back of his head was nearly bald, and his neck and breast were ragged and tattered.

Yes, Corbie was molting, and he had a very unfinished sort of look while the new crop of paint-brushes sprouted out all over him. But it was worth the discomforts of the molt to have the new feather coat, all shiny black; and Corbie was even handsomer than he had been during the summer, when cold days came, and he needed his warm thick suit.

At this time all the wild crows that had nested in that part of the country flew every night from far and wide to the famous crow-roost, not far from a big peach orchard. They came down from the mountain that showed like a long blue ridge against the sky. They flew across a road that looked, on account of the color of the dirt, like a pinkish-red ribbon stretching off and away. They left the river-edge and the fields. Every night they gathered together, a thousand or more of them. Corbie's father and mother were among them, and Corbie's two brothers and two sisters. But Corbie was not with those thousand crows.

No cage held him, and no one prevented his flying whither he wished; but Corbie stayed with the folk who had adopted him. A thousand wild crows might come and go, calling in their flight, but Corbie, though free, chose for his comrades the Brown-eyed Boy and the Blue-eyed Girl.

I thought all along it would be so if they were good to him; and that is why I said, the day he was kidnaped, that you need not be sorry for Corbie—not very.

VIII
ARDEA'S SOLDIER

In years long gone by, soldiers called "knights" used to protect the rights of other people; and, when the weak were in danger, these soldiers went forth to fight for them. They were so brave, these knights of old, that there was nothing that could make them afraid. Dragons even, which looked like crocodiles, with leather wings and terrible snatching claws and fiery eyes and breath that smoked—dragons, even, so the stories go, could not turn a knight away from his path of duty. Mind, I am not telling you that there ever were creatures that looked like that; but certain it is that there were dangers dreadful to meet, and "dragon" is a very good name to call them by.

You know, do you not, that there are soldiers, still, who protect the rights of others; and although we do not commonly call them "knights," they still fight for the weak, and are so brave that dangers as fearsome as dragons, even, cannot scare them.

There was such a soldier in Ardea's camp; and if he had lived in olden days, he would probably have been called "Knight of the Snowy Heron."

Ardea was a bride that spring, and perhaps never was there one much lovelier. Her wedding garment was the purest white; and instead of a veil she wore, draped from her shoulders, snowy plumes of rare beauty, which reached to the bottom of her gown, where the dainty tips curled up a bit, then hung like the finest fringe.

She wore, draped from her shoulders, snowy plumes of rare beauty.

The Soldier watched her as she stood alone at the edge of the water, so small and white and slender against the great cypress trees bearded with Spanish moss, and thought she made a picture he could never forget. And when her mate came out to her, in a white wedding-robe like her own, with its filmy cape of mist-fine plumes, Ardea's Soldier smiled gently, for he loved Heron Camp and shared, in his heart, the joys of their home-coming.

Ardea and her mate took a pleasant trip, looking for a building place at the edge of a swamp. They did not object to neighbors; which was fortunate, as there were so many other herons in the camp that it would have been hard to find a very secret spot for their nest. After looking it over and talking about it a bit, they chose a mangrove bush for their very own. They had never built a house before, but they wasted no time in hunting for a carpenter or teacher, but went to work with a will, just as if they knew how. It was like playing a game of "five-six, pick up sticks"; only they did not lay them straight but in a scraggly criss-cross sort of platform, with big twigs twelve inches long at the bottom and smaller ones on top. Then, when it looked all ready for a nice soft lining, Ardea laid an egg right on the rough sticks. Rather lazy and shiftless, don't you think? or maybe they didn't know any better, poor young things who had never had a home before! Ah, but there was another pair of snowy herons building in the bush next door, and they didn't put in anything soft for their eggs, either; and six or eight bushes farther on, a little blue heron was already sitting on her blue eggs in almost exactly the same sort of nest.

So that is the kind of carpenters herons are! Sticks laid tangled up in a mass is the way they build! Yes, that is all—just some old dead twigs. I mean that is all you could *see*; but never think for a minute that there wasn't something else about that nest; for Ardea and her mate had lined it well with love, and so it was, indeed, a home worth building.

Near Ardea's Home.

In less than a week there were four eggs beneath the white down comforter that Ardea tucked over them; and the little mother was as well pleased as if she had had five, like her neighbors, the other snowy heron and the little blue heron.

If the eggs of the little blue heron were blue, would not those of the snowy herons be pure white? No, the color of eggs does not need to match the color of feathers; and Ardea's eggs and those of her next-bush neighbor were so much like the beautiful blue ones of the little blue heron, that it would be very hard for you to tell one from the other. Perhaps Ardea could not have told her own eggs if she had not remembered where she had built her nest. As it was, she made no mistake, but snuggled cosily over her pretty eggs, doubling up her long slender black legs and her yellow feet as best she could.

If she found it hard to sit there day after day, she made no fuss about it; and probably she really wanted to do that more than anything else just then, since the quiet patience of the most active birds is natural to them when they are brooding their unhatched babies. Then, too, there was her beautiful mate for company and help; for when Ardea needed to leave the nest for food and a change, the father-bird kept house as carefully as need be.

To her next-bush neighbors and the little blue herons Ardea paid no attention, unless, indeed, one of them chanced to come near her own mangrove bush. Then she and her mate would raise the feathers on the top of their heads until they looked rather fierce and bristly, and spread out their filmy capes of dainty plumes in a threatening way. That criss-cross pile of old dead twigs was a dear home after all, being lined, you will remember, with the love of Ardea and her mate; and they both guarded it as well as they were able.

At last the quiet brooding days came to an end, and four funny little herons wobbled about in Ardea's nest. Their long legs and toes stuck out in all directions, and they couldn't seem to help sprawling around. If there had been string or strands of moss or grass in the nest, they would probably have got all tangled up. As it was, they sometimes nearly spilled out, and saved themselves only by clinging to the firm sticks and twigs. So it would seem that their home was a good sort for the needs of their early life, just as it was; and no doubt a heron's nest for a heron is as suitable a building as an oriole's is for an oriole.

That criss-cross pile of old dead twigs was a dear home, and they both guarded it.

It would take some time before the babies of Ardea would be able to straighten up on their long, slim legs and go wading. Until that day came, their father and mother would have to feed them well and often. Now the marsh where the snowy herons went fishing, where the shallow water was a favorite swimming-place for little fishes, was ten miles or more from their nest. Some kinds of herons, perhaps most kinds, are quiet and stately when they hunt, standing still and waiting for their game to come to them, or moving very slowly and carefully. But Ardea and the other snowy herons ran about in a lively way, spying out the little fishes with their bright yellow eyes, and catching them up quickly in their black beaks. After swallowing a supply of food, Ardea took wing and returned across the miles to her young. Standing on the edge of her nest and reaching down with her long neck, she took the bill of one of her babies in her own mouth, and dropped part of what she had swallowed out of her big throat down into his small one. When she had fed her babies and preened her pretty feathers a bit, she was off again on the ten-mile flight; for many a long journey she and her mate must take ere their little ones could feed themselves. But ten miles over and over and over again were as nothing to the love she had for her children; and faithfully as she had brooded her eggs, she now began the task of providing their meals. She seemed so happy each time she returned, that perhaps she was a little bit worried while she was away; but there is no reason to think she really was afraid that any great harm could come to them.

Certainly she was unprepared for what she found when she flew back from her fourth fishing trip. Even when she reached Heron Camp, she did not understand. There are some things it is not given the mind of a bird to know.

She could not know, poor dear, that there were people in the world who coveted her beautiful wedding plumes. Women there were, who wished to make themselves look better by wearing the feathers that Nature had given snowy herons for their very own. And men there were, who thought to make themselves grander in the dress of their organization by walking about with heron plumes waving on their heads. The two kinds of white herons with wonderful plumes that have been put to such uses are called Egrets and Snowy Egrets, and the feathers, when they are stripped from the birds, are called by the French name of *aigrette*.

Now, of course, Ardea could not know about this, or that the Plume-Hunters had come to steal her wedding feathers. But she knew well enough that danger was at hand, and that in times of trouble a mother's place is beside her babies. Her heart beat quickly with a new terror, but she stayed, the brave bird stayed! And all about her the other herons stayed also. They had no way to fight for their lives, and they might have flown far and safely on their strong wings; but none of them would desert the home built with love while the frightened babies were calling to their fathers and mothers.

No, *they* could not fight for their lives, but there was one who could. For danger did not come to Heron Camp without finding Ardea's Soldier at his post.

Now the Plume-Hunters did not have bodies like crocodiles and leather wings, you know; but they were dragons of a sort, for all that, for they carried brutal things in their hands that belched forth smoke and pain and death, and they were cruel of heart, and they had sold themselves to do evil for the sake of the dollars that covetous men and women would pay them for feathers.

Dragons though they were, Ardea's Soldier met them bravely. I like to think how brave he was; for was not the fight he fought a fight for our good old Mother Earth, that she might not lose those beautiful children of hers? If the world should be robbed of Snowy Herons, it would be just so much less lovely, just so much less wonderful. And have they no right to life, since the same Power that gave life to men gave life to them? And when we think about it this way, who seems to have the better right to those plumes— herons, or men and women?

The Soldier believed in Ardea's right to life, believed in it so deeply that he stood alone before the Plume-Hunters and told them that, while he lived, the birds of his camp should also live.

And that is why they killed him—the dragons who were cruel of heart and had sold themselves to do evil for the sake of dollars that covetous men and women would pay for feathers.

Because of his courage and because of the cause for which he died, I think, don't you, that Ardea's Soldier might well be called "Knight of the Snowy Heron."

I said that he was alone, and it is true that no one was there at the camp to help him. But many there were in other places doing their bit in the same good fight. Another soldier, named Theodore Roosevelt, did much for these birds when he was President, by granting them land where no man had a right to touch them; for it makes a true soldier angry when the weak are oppressed, and he said, "It is a disgrace to America that we should permit the sale of aigrettes." Another man, named Woodrow Wilson, whose courage also was so great that he always did what he believed to be right, would not permit, when he was Governor of New Jersey, a company to sell aigrettes in that State; he said, "I think New Jersey can get along without blood-money."

Many another great man, besides, served the cause of Ardea. So many, in fact, that there is not room here to tell about them all. But there is room to say that the children helped. For, you know, every Junior Audubon Society sends money to the National Association of Audubon Societies—not much, but a little; and when the Knight of the Snowy Heron was killed, that little helped the National Association to hire another soldier to take his place. Now, think of that! There was another soldier who so believed in the Herons' right to life and plumage, that he was ready to protect them though it meant certain danger to himself!

Yes, there is to this very day a soldier at Heron Camp. Do you know a way to keep him safe? Why, you children of America can do it if you will, and it need not cost one of you a penny. You can do it with your minds. For if every girl makes up her mind for good and all that she will never wear a feather that costs a bird its life; and if every boy makes up his mind for good and all that he will never be a feather-hunting dragon—why there will not be *anybody* growing up in America to harm Ardea, will there? You can keep the Soldier of Heron Camp safe by just wishing it! That sounds wonderful as a fairy story come true, does it not? And like the knight in some old fairy tale, could not Ardea's new Soldier "live happily forever after"?

IX
THE FLYING CLOWN

There are many accounts of the flying clown, in books, nearly all of which refer to him as bull-bat or nighthawk, and a member of the Goatsucker or Nightjar family. But he wasn't a bull and he wasn't a bat and he wasn't a hawk and he wasn't a jar; and he flew more by day than by night, and he never, never milked a goat in all his life. So for the purposes of this story we may as well give him a name to suit ourselves, and call him Mis Nomer.

He was a poor skinny little thing, but you would not have guessed it to see him; for he always wore a loose fluffy coat, which made him look bigger and plumper than he really was. It was a gray and brown and creamy buff-and-white sort of coat, quite mottled, with a rather plain, nearly black, back. It was trimmed with white, there being a white stripe near the end of the coat-tail, a big, fine, V-shaped white place under his chin that had something the look of a necktie, and a bar of white reaching nearly across the middle of each wing.

These bars would have made you notice his long, pointed wings if he had been near you, and they were well worth noticing; for besides just flying with them,—which was wonderful enough, as he was a talented flier,—he used them in a sort of gymnastic stunt he was fond of performing in the springtime.

Perhaps he did it to show off. I do not know. Certainly he had as good a right to be proud of his accomplishments as a turkey or a peacock that spreads its tail, or a boy who walks on his hands. Maybe a better right, for they have solid earth to strut upon and run no risks, while Mis did his whole trick in the air. It was a kind of acrobatic feat, though he had no gymnasium with bars or rings or tight rope, and there was no canvas stretched to catch him if he fell. A circus, with tents, and a gate-keeper to take your ticket, would have been lucky if it could have hired Mis to show his skill for money.

But Mis couldn't be hired. Not he! He was a free, wild clown, performing only under Mother Nature's tent of wide-arched sky. If you wanted to see him, you could—ticket or no ticket. That was nothing to him; for Mis, the wild clown of the air, had no thought either of money or fame among people.

Far, far up, he flew, hither and yon, in a matter-of-fact-enough way; and then of a sudden, with wings half-closed, he dropped toward the earth. Could he stop such speed, or must he strike and kill himself in his fall? Down, down he plunged; and then, at last, he made a sound as if he groaned a loud, deep "boom."

The Flying Clown.

But just at the moment of this sound he was turning, and then, the first anyone knew, he was flying up gayly, quite gayly. Then it wasn't a groan of fear? Mis afraid! Why the rascal had but to move his wings this way and that, and go up instead of down. He might be within a second of dashing himself to death against the ground, but so sure were his wings and so strong his muscles, that a second was time and to spare for him to stop and turn and rise again toward the safe height from which he dived. A fine trick that! The fun of the plunge, and then the quick jerk at the end that sent the wind groaning against and between the feathers of his wings, with a "boom" loud and sudden enough to startle anyone within hearing.

Yes, you might have seen the little clown at his tricks without a ticket at the wild-circus gate, for all he cared or knew. What did the children of men matter to him? Had not his fathers and grandfathers and great-grandfathers given high-air circus performances of a springtime, in the days when bison and passenger pigeons inherited their full share of the earth, before our fathers and grandfathers and great-grandfathers had even seen America?

Was it, then, just for the joy of the season that he played in the air, or was there, after all, someone besides himself to be pleased with the sport? Who knows whether the little acrobat was showing his mate what a splendid fellow he was, how strong of wing and skillful in the tricks of flight? Be that as it may, the mate of Mis was satisfied in some way or other, and went with him on a voyage of discovery one afternoon, when the sky was nicely cloudy and the light pleasantly dull.

Now, like all good parents, Mis and his mate were a bit particular about what sort of neighborhood they should choose for their home; for the bringing up of a family, even if it is a small one, is most important.

A peaceful place and a sunny exposure they must have; there must be good hunting near at hand; and one more thing, too, was necessary. Now, the house-lot they finally decided upon met all four of these needs, though it sounds like a joke to tell you where it was. But then, when a clown goes merrily forth to find him a home, we must not be surprised if he is funny about it. It was where the sun could shine upon it; though how Mis and his mate knew that, all on a dull, dark afternoon, I'm sure I can't tell. Maybe because there wasn't a tree in sight. And as for peace, it was as undisturbed as a deserted island. It was, in fact, a sort of island in a sea of air, and at certain times of the day and night there was game enough in this sea to satisfy even such hunters as they.

Perhaps they chuckled cosily together when they decided to take their peace and sunshine on the flat roof of a very high building in a very large city. Their house-lot was covered with pebbles, and it suited them exactly. So well that they moved in, just as it was.

Yes, those two ridiculous birds set up housekeeping without any house. Mother Nomer just settled herself on the bare pebbles in a satisfied way, and that was all there was to it. Not a stick or a wisp of hay or a feather to mark the place! And as she sat there quietly, a queer thing happened. She disappeared from sight. As long as she didn't move, she couldn't be seen. Her dappled feathers didn't look like a bird. They looked like the light and dark of the pebbles of the flat roof. Ah, so *that* was the one thing more that was necessary for her home, besides sunshine and peace and good hunting. It must be where she could sit and not show; where she could hide by just looking like what was near her, like a sand-colored grasshopper on the sand in the sun,[2] or a walking-stick on a twig,[2] or a butterfly on the bark of a tree.[2]

Yes, Mis's mate knew, in some natural wise way of her own, the secret of making use of what we call her "protective coloration." This is one of the very most important secrets Mother Nature has given her children, and many use it—not birds alone, but beasts and insects also. They use it in their own wild way and think nothing about it. We say that it is their instinct that leads them to choose places where they cannot easily be seen. If you do not understand exactly what instinct is, do not feel worried, for there are some things about that secret of Mother Nature that even the wisest men in the world have not explained. But this we do know, that when her instincts led Mother Nomer to choose the pebbly roof as a background for her mottled feathers, she did just naturally very much the same thing that the soldiers in the world-war did when they made use of great guns painted to look like things they were not, and ships painted to look like the waves beneath them and the clouds in the sky above. Only, the soldiers did not use their protective coloration naturally and by instinct. They did this by taking thought; and very proud they felt, too, of being able to do this by hard study. They talked about it a great deal and the French taught the world a new word, *camouflage*, to call it by. And their war-time camouflage *was* wonderful, even though it was only a clumsy imitation of what Mother Nature did when the feathers of Mother Nomer were made to grow dappled like little blotches of light and dark; or, to put it the other way about, when the bird was led, by her instinct, to choose for the nesting-time a place where she did not show.

Of course, it was not just the gravel on the flat roof that would match her feathers; for there isn't a house in the land that is nearly so old as one thousand years, and birds of this sort have been building much longer than that. No, so far as color went, Mother Nomer might have chosen a spot in an open field, where there were little broken sticks or stones to give it a mottled look—such a place, indeed, as her ancestors used to find for their nesting in the old days when there were no houses. Such a place, too, as most of this kind of bird still seek; for not all of them, by any means, are roof-dwellers in cities.

Our bird with the dappled feathers, however, sat in one little spot on that large roof for about sixteen days and nights, with time enough off now and then to get food and water, and to exercise her wings. When she was away, Mis came and sat on the same spot. If you had been there to see them come and go, you would have wondered why they cared about that particular spot. It looked like the rest of the sunny roof—just little humps of light and dark. Ah, yes! but two of those little humps of light and dark were not pebbles: they were eggs; and if you couldn't have found them, Mis and his mate could, though I think even they had to remember where they were instead of eye-spying them.

By the time sixteen days were over, there were no longer eggs beneath the fluffy feathers that had covered them. Instead, there were two little balls of down, though you couldn't have seen them either, unless you had been about near enough to touch them; for the downy children of Mis were as dappled as his mate and her eggs, and they had, from the moment of their hatching, the instinct for keeping still if danger came near.

Peaceful enough, indeed, had been the brooding days.

Peaceful enough, indeed, had been the brooding days of Mother Nomer. Something of the noise and bustle, to be sure, of the city streets came up to her; but that was from far below, and things far off are not worth worrying about. Sometimes, too, the sound of voices floated out from the upper windows of the building, quite near; but the birds soon became used to that.

When the twins were but a few days old, however, their mother had a real scare. A man came up to take down some electric wires that had been fastened not far from the spot that was the Nomer home. He tramped heavily about, throwing down his tools here and there, and whistling loudly as he worked. All this frightened little Mother Nomer. There is no doubt about that, for her heart beat more and more quickly. But she didn't budge. She couldn't. It was a part of her camouflage trick to sit still in danger. The greater the danger, the stiller to sit! She even kept her eyes nearly shut, until, when the man had cut the last and nearest end of wire and put all his things together in a pile ready to take down, he came to look over the edge of the roof-wall. As he bent to do this, he brushed suddenly against her.

Then Mother Nomer sprang into the air; and the man jumped, in such surprise that, had it not been for the wall, he would have fallen from the roof. It would be hard to tell which was the more startled for a moment—man or bird. But Mother Nomer did not fly far. She fell back to the roof some distance from her precious babies and fluttered pitifully about, her wings and tail spread wide and dragging as she moved lamely. She did not look like a part of the pebbly roof now. She showed plainly, for she was moving. She looked like a wounded bird, and the man, thinking he must have hurt her in some way, followed her to pick her up and see what the trouble was. Three times he almost got her. Almost, but not quite. Crippled as she seemed, she could still fumble and flutter just out of reach; and when at last the man had followed her to a corner of the roof far from her young, Mother Nomer sprang up, and spreading her long, pointed wings, took flight, whole and sound as a bird need be.

The man understood and laughed. He laughed at himself for being fooled. For it wasn't the first time a bird had tricked him so. Once, when he was a country boy, a partridge, fluttering as if broken-winged, had led him through the underbrush of the wood-lot; and once a bird by the river-side stumbled on before him, crying piteously, "Pete! Pete! Pete-weet!" and once—Why, yes, he should have remembered that this is the trick of many a mother-bird when danger threatens her young.

So he went back, with careful step, to where he had been before. He looked this way and that. There was no nest. He saw no young. The little Nomer twins were not the son and daughter of Mis, the clown, and Mother Nomer, the trick cripple, for nothing! They sat there, the little rascals, right before his eyes, and budged not; they could practice the art of camouflage, too.

The little rascals could practise the art of camouflage.

But as he stood and looked, a wistful light came into the eyes of the man. It had been many years since he had found nesting birds and watched the ways of them. His memory brought old pictures back to him. The crotch in the tree, where the robin had plastered her nest, modeling the mud with her feathered breast; the brook-edge willows, where the blackbirds built; the meadow, with its hidden homes of bobolinks; and the woods where the whip-poor-wills called o' nights. His thoughts made a boy of him again, and he forgot everything else in the world in his wish to see the little birds he felt sure must be among the pebbles before him. So he crept about carefully, here and there, and at last came upon the children of Mis. He picked up the fluffy little balls of down and snuggled them gently in his big hands for a moment. Then he put them back to their safe roof, and, gathering up his tools, went on his way, whistling a merry tune remembered from the days when he trudged down Long-ago Lane to the pasture, for his father's cows. Late of afternoon it used to be, while the nighthawks dashed overhead in their air-hunts, showing the white spots in their wings that looked like holes, and sometimes making him jump as they dropped and turned, with a sudden "boom."

No sooner had the sound of his whistle gone from the roof, than Mother Nomer came back to her houseless home—any spot doing as well as another, now that the twins were hatched and able to walk about. As she called her babies to her and tucked them under her feathers, her heart still beating quickly with the excitement of her scare, it would be easy to guess from the dear way of her cuddling that it isn't a beautiful woven cradle or quaint walls of clay that matter most in the life of young birds, but the loving care that is given them. In this respect the young orioles, swinging in their hammock among the swaying tips of the elm tree, and the children of Eve and Petro, in their wonderful brick mansion, were no better off than the twins of Mis and Mother Nomer.

Busy indeed was Mis in the twilights that followed the hatching of his children; and, though he was as much in the air as ever, it was not the fun of frolic and clownish tricks that kept him there. For, besides his own keen appetite, he had now the hunger of the twins to spur him on. Such a hunter as he was in those days! Why, he caught a thousand mosquitos on one trip; and meeting a swarm of flying ants, thought nothing at all of gobbling up five hundred before he stopped. Countless flies went down his throat. And when the big, brown bumping beetles, with hard, shiny wing-covers on their backs and soft, fuzzy velvet underneath, flew out at dusk, twenty or thirty of them, as likely as not, would make a luncheon for Mis the clown. For he was lean and hungry, and he ate and ate and ate; but he never grew fat. He hunted zigzag through the twilight of the evening and the twilight of the dawn. When the nights were bright and game was plenty, he hunted zigzag through the moonlight. When the day was dull and insects were on the wing, he hunted, though it was high noon. And many a midnight rambler going home from the theatre looked up, wondering what made the darting shadows, and saw Mis and his fellows dashing busily above where the night-insects were hovering about the electric lights of the city streets. He hunted long and he hunted well; but so keen was his appetite and so huge the hunger of his twins, that it took the mother, too, to keep the meals provided in the Nomer home.

I think they were never unhappy about it, for there is a certain satisfaction in doing well what we can do; and there is no doubt that these birds were made to be hunters. Mis and his kind swept the air, of course, because they and their young were hungry; but the game they caught, had it gone free to lay its myriad eggs, would have cost many a farmer a fortune in sprays to save his crops, and would have added untold discomfort to dwellers in country and city alike.

Although Mis, under his feathers, was much smaller than one would think to look at him, there were several large things about him besides his appetite. His mouth was almost huge, and reached way around to the sides of his head under his eyes. It opened up more like the mouth of a frog or a toad than like that of most birds. When he hunted he kept it yawning wide open, so that it made a trap for many an unlucky insect that flew straight in, without ever knowing what happened to it when it disappeared down the great hollow throat, into a stomach so enormous that it hardly seems possible that a bird less than twice the size of Mis could own it.

There were other odd things about him, too—for instance, the comb he wore on his middle toe-nail. What he did with it, I can't say. He didn't seem to do very much with his feet anyway. They were rather feeble little things, and he never used them in carrying home anything he caught. He didn't even use them as most birds do when they stop to rest; for, instead of sitting on a twig when he was not flying, he would settle as if lying down. Sometimes he stayed on a large level branch, not cross-wise like most birds, but the long way; and when he did that, he looked like a humpy knot on the branch. When there were no branches handy, he would use a rail or a log or a wall, or even the ground; but wherever he settled himself, he looked like a blotch of light and dark, and one could gaze right at him without noticing that a bird was there. That was the way Mother Nomer did, too—clowns both of them and always ready for the wonderful game of camouflage!

They had remarkable voices. There seemed to be just one word to their call. I am not going to tell you what that word is. There is a reason why I am not. The reason is, that I do not know. To be sure, I have heard nighthawks say it every summer for years, but I can't say it myself. It is a very funny word, but you will have to get one of them to speak it for you!

They came by all their different kinds of queerness naturally enough, Mis and Mother Nomer did, for it seemed to run in the family to be peculiar, and all their relatives had oddities of one kind or another. Take Cousin Whip-poor-will, who wears whiskers, for instance; and Cousin Chuck-will's widow, who wears whiskers that branch. You could tell from their very names that they would do uncommon things. And as for their more distant relatives, the Hummingbirds and Chimney Swifts, it would take a story apiece as long as this to begin to tell of their strange doings. But it is a nice, likable sort of queerness they all have; so very interesting, too, that we enjoy them the better for it.

There is one more wonderful thing yet that Mis and his mate did—and their twins with them; for before this happened, the children had grown to be as big as their parents, and a bit plumper, perhaps, though not enough to be noticed under their feathers. Toward the end of a pleasant summer, they joined a company of their kind, a sort of traveling circus, and went south for the winter. Just what performances they gave along the way, I did not hear; but with a whole flock of flying clowns on the wing, it seems likely that they had a gay time of it altogether!

FOOTNOTES:

[2] See *Hexapod Stories*, pages 4, 110, 126.

X
THE LOST DOVE

One Thousand Dollars ($1000) Reward

That is the prize that has been offered for a nesting pair of Passenger Pigeons. No one has claimed the money yet, and it would be a great adventure, don't you think, to seek that nest? If you find it, you must not disturb it, you know, or take the eggs or the young, or frighten the father- or mother-bird; for the people who offered all that money did not want dead birds to stuff for a museum, but hoped that someone might tell them where there were live wild ones nesting.

You see the news had got about that the dove that is called Passenger Pigeon was lost. No one could believe this at first, because there had been so very many—more than a thousand, more than a million, more than a billion. How could more than a billion doves be lost?

They were such big birds, too—a foot and a half long from tip of beak to tip of tail, and sometimes even longer. Why, that is longer than the tame pigeons that walk about our city streets. How could doves as large as that be lost, so that no one could find a pair, not even for one thousand dollars to pay him for the time it took to hunt?

Their colors were so pretty—head and back a soft, soft blue; neck glistening with violet, red, and gold; underneath, a wonderful purple red fading into violet shades, and then into bluish white. Who would not like to seek, for the love of seeing so beautiful a bird, even though no one paid a reward in money?

Shall we go, then, to Kentucky? For 'twas there the man named Audubon once saw them come in flocks to roost at night. They kept coming from sunset till after midnight, and their numbers were so great that their wings, even while still a long way off, made a sound like a gale of wind; and when close to, the noise of the birds was so loud that men could not hear one another speak, even though they stood near and shouted. The place where Audubon saw these pigeons was in a forest near the Green River; and there were so many that they filled the trees over a space forty miles long and more than three miles wide. They perched so thickly that the branches of the great trees broke under their weight, and went crashing to the ground; and their roosting-place looked as if a tornado had rushed through the forest.

Must there not be wild pigeons, yet, roosting in Kentucky—some small flock, perhaps, descended from the countless thousands seen by Audubon? No, not one of all these doves is left, they tell us, in the woods in that part of the country. The rush of their wings has been stilled and their evening uproar has been silenced. Men may now walk beside the Green River, and hear each other though they speak in whispers.

Would you like to seek the dove in Michigan in May? For there it was, and then it was, that these wild pigeons nested, so we are told by people who saw them, by hundreds of thousands, or even millions. They built in trees of every sort, and sometimes as many as one hundred nests were made in a single tree. Almost every tree on one hundred thousand acres would have at least one nest. The lowest ones were so near the ground that a man could reach them with his hand.

Suppose you should find just one pair.

Suppose you should find, next May, just one pair nesting. Sire Dove, we think from what we have read, would help bring some twigs, and Dame Dove would lay them together in a criss-cross way, so that they would make a floor of sticks, sagging just a little in the middle. As soon as the floor of twigs was firm enough, so that an egg would not drop through, Dame Dove would put one in the shallow sagging place in the middle. It would be a white egg, very much like those our tame pigeons lay; and, because there would be no thick soft warm rug of dried grass on the floor, you could probably see it right through the nest, if you should stand underneath and look up. But you couldn't see it long, because, almost as soon as it was laid, Dame Dove would tuck the feather comforter she carried on her breast so cosily about that precious egg, that it would need no other padding to keep it warm. She would stay there, the faithful mother, from about two o'clock each afternoon until nine or ten o'clock the next morning. She would not leave for one minute, to eat or get a drink of water. Then, about nine or ten o'clock each morning, Sire Dove would slip onto the nest just as she moved off, and they would make the change so quickly that the egg could not even get cool. That one very dear egg would need two birds to take care of it, one always snuggling it close while the other ate and flew about and drank.

So they would sit, turn and turn about, for fourteen days. All this while they would be very gentle with each other, saying softly, "Coo-coo," something as tame pigeons do, only in shorter notes, or calling, "Kee-kee-kee." And sometimes Sire Dove would put his beak to that of his nesting mate and feed her, very likely, as later they would feed their young. For when the two weeks' brooding should be over, there would be a funny, homely, sprawling, soft and wobbly baby dove within the nest.

The father and mother of him would still have much to do, it seems; for hatching a dove out of an egg is only the easier half of the task. The wobbly baby must be brought up to become a dove of grace and beauty. That would take food.

But you must not think to see Sire and Dame Dove come flying home with seeds or nuts or fruit or grain or earthworms or insects in their beaks. What else, then, could they bring? Well, nothing at all, indeed, in their beaks; for the food of a baby dove requires especial preparation. It has to be provided for him in the crop of his parent. So Dame Dove would come with empty beak but full crop, and the baby would be fed. Just exactly how, I have not seen written by those people who saw a million Passenger Pigeons. Perhaps they did not stop to notice.

However, if you will watch a tame pigeon feed its young, you can guess how a wild one would do it. A tame mother-pigeon that I am acquainted with comes to her young (*she* has two) and, standing in or beside the nest, opens her beak very wide. One of her babies reaches up as far as he can stretch his neck and puts his beak inside his mother's mouth. He tucks it in at one side and crowds in his head as far as he can push it. Then the mother makes a sort of pumping motion, and pumps up soft baby food from her crop, and he swallows it. Sometimes he keeps his beak in his mother's mouth for as long as five minutes; and if anything startles her and she pulls away, the hungry little fellow scolds and whines and whimpers in a queer voice, and reaches out with his teasing wings, and flaps them against her breast, stretching up with his beak all the while and feeling for a chance to poke his head into her mouth again. And often, do you know, his twin sister gets her beak in one side of Mother Pigeon's mouth while he is feeding at the other side, and Mother just stands there and pumps and pumps. The two comical little birds, with feet braced and necks stretched up as far as they can reach, and their heads crowded as far in as they can push them, look so funny they would make you laugh to see them. Then, the next meal Father Pigeon feeds them the same way, usually one at a time, but often both together.

Now, I think, don't you, because that is the way tame Father and Mother Pigeon serve breakfast and dinner and supper and luncheons in between whiles to their tame twins, that wild Dame and Sire Dove would give food in very much the same way to their one wild baby? It might not be exactly the same, because tame pigeons and wild Passenger Pigeons are not the same kind of doves; but they are cousins of a sort, which means that they must have some of the same family habits.

If you should find a nest in Michigan in May, perhaps you can learn more about these matters, and watch to see whether, when the baby dove is all feathered out, Dame or Sire Dove pushes it out of the nest even before it can fly, though it is fat enough to be all right until it gets so hungry it learns to find food for itself. Perhaps you can watch, too, to see why Dame and Sire Dove seem to be in such a hurry to have their first baby taking care of himself. Is it because they are ready to build another nest right straight away, or would Dame Dove lay another egg in the same nest? Tame Mother Pigeon often lays two more eggs in the next nest-box even before her twins are out of their nest. Then you may be sure Father and Mother Pigeon have a busy time of it feeding their eldest twins, while they brood the two eggs in which their younger twins are growing.

It would be very pleasant if you could watch a pair of Passenger Pigeons and find out all these things about them. *If you could!* But I said only "perhaps," because the people who know most about the matter say that Michigan has lost more than a million, or possibly more than a billion, doves. They say that, if you should walk through all the woods in Michigan, you would not hear one single Passenger Pigeon call, "Kee-kee-kee" to his mate, or hear one pair talk softly together, saying, "Coo-coo." There are sticks and twigs enough for their nests lying about; but through all the lonesome woods, so we are told, there is not one Sire Dove left to bring them to his Dame; and never, never, never will there be another nest like the millions there used to be.

Through all the lonesome woods there is not one dove.

Well, then, if we cannot find them at sunset in their roosting-place in Kentucky or in their nests in Michigan in May, shall we give up the quest for the lost doves? Or shall we still keep hold of our courage and our hope and try elsewhere?

Surely, if there are any of these birds anywhere, they must eat food! Shall we seek them at some feeding-place? This might be everywhere in North America, from the Atlantic Ocean as far west as the Great Plains. That is, everywhere in all these miles where the things they liked to eat are growing. So, if you keep out of the Atlantic Ocean, and get someone to show you where the Great Plains are, you might look—*almost anywhere*. Why, many of you would not need to take a steam-train or even a trolley-car. You could walk there. Most of you could. You could walk to a place where they used to stop to feed. Those that were behind in the great flock flew over the heads of all the others, and so were in front for a while. In that way they all had a chance at a well-spread picnic ground. Yes, you could easily walk to a place where that used to happen—most of you could.

Do you know where acorns grow, or beechnuts, or chestnuts? Well, Passenger Pigeons used to come there to eat, for they were very fond of nuts! Do you know where elm trees grow wild along some riverway, or where pine trees live? Oh! that is where these birds used sometimes to get their breakfasts, when the trees had scattered their seeds. Do you know a tree that has a seed about the right size and shape for a knife at a doll's tea-party? Yes, that's the maple; and many and many a party the Passenger Pigeons used to have wherever they could find these cunning seed-knives. Only they didn't use them to cut things with. They ate them up as fast as ever they could.

Have you ever picked wild berries? Why, more than likely Passenger Pigeons have picked other berries there or thereabouts before your day!

Do you know a place where the wild rice grows? Ah, so did the Passenger Pigeons, once upon a time!

But if you know none of these places, even then you can stand near where the flocks used to fly when they were on their journeys. All of you who live between the Atlantic Ocean and the Great Plains can go to the door or a window of the house you live in and point to the sky and think: "Once so many Passenger Pigeons flew by that the sound of their wings was like the sound of thunder, and they went through the air faster than a train on a track, and the numbers in their flocks were so many that they hid the sun like great thick clouds."

When you do that, some of you will doubtless see birds flying over; but we fear that not even one of you will see even one Passenger Pigeon in its flight.

What happened to the countless millions is recorded in so many books that it need not be written again in this one. This story will tell you just one more thing about these strange and wonderful birds, and that is that no *child* who reads this story is in any way to blame because the dove is lost. What boy or girl is not glad to think, when some wrong has been done or some mistake has been made, "It's not *my* fault"?

Once, so many flew by, that the sound of their wings was like the sound of thunder.

Even though this bird is gone forever and forever and forever, there are many other kinds living among us. If old Mother Earth has been robbed of some of her children, she still has many more—many wonderful and beautiful living things. And that she may keep them safe, she needs your help; for boys and girls are her children, too, and the power lies in your strong hands and your courageous hearts and your wise brains to help save some of the most wonderful and fairest of other living things. And what one among you all, I wonder, will not be glad to think that *you* help keep the world beautiful, when you leave the water-lilies floating on the pond; that it is the same as if *you* sow the seeds in wild gardens, when you leave the cardinal flowers glowing on the banks and the fringed gentians lending their blue to the marshes. For the life of the world, whether it flies through the air or grows in the ground, is greatly in your care; and though you may never win a prize of money for finding the dove that other people lost, there is a reward of joy ready for anyone who can look at our good old Mother Earth and say, "It will not be *my* fault if, as the years go by, you lose your birds and flowers."

And it would be, don't you think, one of the greatest of adventures to seek and find and help keep safe such of these as are in danger, that they may not, like the dove, be lost?

XI
LITTLE SOLOMON OTUS

Oh, the wise, wise look of him, with his big round eyes and his very Roman nose! He had sat in a golden silence throughout that dazzling day; but when the kindly moon sent forth a gentler gleam, he spoke, and the speech of little Solomon Otus was as silver. A quivering, quavering whistle thrilled through the night, and all who heard the beginning listened to the end of his song.

It was a night and a place for music. The mellow light lay softly over the orchard tree, on an old branch of which little Solomon sat mooning himself before his door. He could see, not far away, the giant chestnut trees that shaded the banks of a little ravine; and hear the murmuring sound of Shanty Creek, where Natal[3] grew up, and where her grandchildren now played hide-and-seek. Near at hand stood a noble oak, with a big dead branch at the top that was famous the country round as a look-out post for hawks and crows; and maybe an eagle now and then had used it, in years gone by.

But hawk and crow were asleep, and toads were trilling a lullaby from the pond, while far, far off in the heart of the woods, a whip-poor-will called once, twice, and again.

Solomon loved the dusk. His life was fullest then and his sight was keenest. His eyes were wide open, and he could see clearly the shadow of the leaves when the wind moved them lightly from time to time. He was at ease in the great night-world, and master of many a secret that sleepy-eyed day-folk never guess. As he shook out his loose, soft coat and breathed the cool air, he felt the pleasant tang of a hunger that has with it no fear of famine.

Once more he sent his challenge through the moonlight with quivering, quavering voice, and some who heard it loved the darkness better for this spirit of the night, and some shivered as if with dread. For Solomon had sounded his hunting call, and, as with the baying of hounds or the tune of a hunter's horn, one ear might find music in the note and another hear only a wail.

Then, silent as a shadow, he left his branch. Solomon, a little lone hunter in the dark, was off on the chase. Whither he went or what he caught, there was no sound to tell, until, suddenly, one quick squeak way over beside the corn-crib might have notified a farmer that another mouse was gone. But the owner of the corn-crib was asleep, and dreaming, more than likely, that the cat, which was at that moment disturbing a pair of meadow bobolinks, was somehow wholly to be thanked for the scarcity of mice about the place.

Oh, the wise, wise look of him.

Solomon was not wasteful about his food. He swallowed his evening breakfast whole. That is, he swallowed all but the tail, which was fairly long and stuck out of his mouth for some time, giving him rather a queer two-tailed look, one at each end! But there was no one about to laugh at him, and it was, in some respects, an excellent way to make a meal. For one thing, it saved him all trouble of cutting up his food; and then, too, there was no danger of his overeating, for he could tell that he had had enough as long as there wasn't room for the tail. And after the good nutritious parts of his breakfast were digested, he had a comfortable way of spitting out the skin and bones all wadded together in a tidy pellet. An owl is not the only kind of bird, by any means, that has a habit of spitting out hard stuff that is swallowed with the food. A crow tucks away many a discarded cud of that sort; and even the thrush, half an hour or so after a dainty fare of wild cherries, taken whole, drops from his bill to the ground the pits that have been squeezed out of the fruit by the digestive mill inside of him.

After his breakfast, which he ate alone in the evening starlight and moonlight, Solomon passed an enjoyable night; for that world, which to most of us is lost in darkness and in sleep, is full of lively interest to an owl. Who, indeed, would not be glad to visit his starlit kingdom, with eyesight keen enough to see the folded leaves of clover like little hands in prayer—a kingdom with byways sweet with the scent and mellow with the beauty of waking primrose? Who would not welcome, for one wonderful night, the gift of ears that could hear the sounds which to little Solomon were known and understood, but many of which are lost in deafness to our dull ears?

Of course, it may be that Solomon never noticed that clovers fold their leaves by night, or that primroses are open and fragrant after dusk. For he was an owl, and not a person, and his thoughts were not the thoughts of man. But for all that they were wise thoughts—wise as the look of his big round eyes; and many things he knew which are unguessed secrets to dozy day-folk.

He was a successful hunter, and he had a certain sort of knowledge about the habits of the creatures he sought. He seldom learned where the day birds slept, for he did not find motionless things. But he knew well enough that mice visited the corn-crib, and where their favorite runways came out into the open. He knew where the cutworms crept out of the ground and feasted o' nights in the farmer's garden. He knew where the big brown beetles hummed and buzzed while they munched greedily of shade-tree leaves. And he knew where little fishes swam near the surface of the water.

So he hunted on silent wings the bright night long; and though he did not starve himself, as we can guess from what we know about his breakfast of rare mouse-steak, still, the tenderest and softest delicacies he took home to five fine youngsters, who welcomed their father with open mouths and eager appetite. Though he made his trips as quickly as he could, he never came too soon to suit them—the hungry little rascals.

Solomon knew the runways of the mice.

They were cunning and dear and lovable. Even a person could see that, to look at them. It is not surprising that their own father was fond enough of them to give them the greater part of the game he caught. He had, indeed, been interested in them before he ever saw them—while they were still within the roundish white eggshells, and did not need to be fed because there was food enough in the egg to last them all the days until they hatched.

Yes, many a time he had kept those eggs warm while Mrs. Otus was away for a change; and many a time, too, he stayed and kept her company when she was there to care for them herself. Now, it doesn't really need two owls at the same time to keep a few eggs warm. Of course not! So why should little Solomon have sat sociably cuddled down beside her? Perhaps because he was fond of her and liked her companionship. It would have been sad, indeed, if he had not been happy in his home, for he was an affectionate little fellow and had had some difficulty in winning his mate. There had been, early in their acquaintance, what seemed to Solomon a long time during which she would not even speak to him. Why, 'tis said he had to bow to her as many as twenty or thirty times before she seemed even to notice that he was about. But those days were over for good and all, and Mrs. Otus was a true comrade for Solomon as well as a faithful little mother. Together they made a happy home, and were quite charming in it.

They could be brave, too, when courage was needed, as they gave proof the day that a boy wished he hadn't climbed up and stuck his hand in at their door-hole, to find out what was there. While Mrs. Otus spread her feathers protectingly over her eggs, Solomon lay on his back, and, reaching up with beak and clutching claws, fought for the safety of his family. In the heat of the battle he hissed, whereupon the boy retreated, badly beaten, but proudly boasting of an adventure with some sort of animal that felt like a wildcat and sounded like a snake.

Besides, courage when needed, health, affection, good-nature, and plenty of food were enough to keep a family of owls contented. To be sure, some folk might not have been so well satisfied with the way the household was run. A crow, I feel quite sure, would not have considered the place fit to live in. Mrs. Otus was not, indeed, a tidy housekeeper. The floor was dirty—very dirty—and was never slicked up from one week's end to another. But then, Solomon didn't mind. He was used to it. Mrs. Otus was just like his own mother in that respect; and it might have worried him a great deal to have to keep things spick and span after the way he had been brought up. Why, the beautiful white eggshell he hatched out of was dirty when he pipped it, and never in all his growing-up days did he see his mother or father really clean house. So it is no wonder he was rather shiftless and easy-going. Neither of them had shown what might be called by some much ambition when they went house-hunting early that spring; for although the place they chose had been put into fairly good repair by rather an able carpenter,—a woodpecker,—still, it had been lived in before, and might have been improved by having some of the rubbish picked up and thrown out. But do you think Solomon spent any of his precious evenings that way? No, nor Mrs. Otus either. They moved in just as it was, in the most happy-go-lucky sort of way.

Well, whatever a crow or other particular person might think of that nest, we should agree that a father and mother owl must be left to manage affairs for their young as Nature has taught them; and if those five adorable babies of Solomon didn't prove that the way they were brought up was an entire success from an owlish point of view, I don't know what could.

Those five adorable babies of Solomon.

Take them altogether, perhaps you could not find a much more interesting family than the little Otuses. As to size and shape, they were as much alike as five peas in a pod; but for all that, they looked so different that it hardly seemed possible that they could be own brothers and sisters. For one of the sons of Solomon and two of his daughters had gray complexions, while the other son and daughter were reddish brown. Now Solomon and Mrs. Otus were both gray, except, of course, what white feathers and black streaks were mixed up in their mottlings and dapples; so it seems strange enough to see two of their children distinctly reddish. But, then, one never can tell just what color an owl of this sort will be, anyway. Solomon himself, though gray, was the son of a reddish father and a gray mother, and he had one gray brother and two reddish sisters: while Mrs. Otus, who had but one brother and one sister, was the only gray member of her family. Young or old, summer or winter, Solomon and Mrs. Otus were gray, though, young or old, summer or winter, their fathers had both been of a reddish complexion.

Now this sort of variation in color you can readily see is altogether a different matter from the way Father Goldfinch changes his feathers every October for a winter coat that looks much the same as that of Mother Goldfinch and his young daughters; and then changes every spring to a beautiful yellow suit, with black-and-white trimmings and a black cap, for the summer. It is different, too, from the color-styles of Bob the Vagabond, who merely wears off the dull tips of his winter feathers, and appears richly garbed in black and white, set off with a lovely bit of yellow, for his gay summer in the north. Again, it is something quite different from the color-fashions of Larie, who was not clothed in a beautiful white garment and soft gray mantle, like his father's and mother's, until he was quite grown up.

No, the complexion of Solomon and his sons and daughters was a different matter altogether, because it had nothing whatever to do with season of the year, or age, or sex. But for all that it was not different from the sort of color-variations that Mother Nature gives to many of her children; and you may meet now and again examples of the same sort among flowers, and insects, and other creatures, too.

But, reddish or gray, it made no difference to Solomon and Mrs. Otus. They had no favorites among their children, but treated them all alike, bringing them food in abundance: not only enough to keep them happy the night long, but laying up a supply in the pantry, so that the youngsters might have luncheons during the day.

Although Solomon had night eyes, he was not blind by day. He passed the brightest hours quietly for the most part, dozing with both his outer eyelids closed, or sometimes sitting with those open and only the thin inner lid drawn sidewise across his eye. It seems strange to think of his having three eyelids; but, then, perhaps we came pretty near having a third one ourselves; for there is a little fold tucked down at the inner corner, which might have been a third lid that could move across the eye sidewise, if it had grown bigger. And sometimes, of a dazzling day in winter, when the sun is shining on the glittering snow, such a thin lid as Solomon had might be very comfortable, even for our day eyes, and save us the trouble of wearing colored glasses.

He passed the brightest hours dozing.

Lively as Solomon was by night, all he asked during the day was peace and quiet. He had it, usually. It was seldom that even any of the wild folk knew where his nest was; and when he spent the day outside, in some shady place, he didn't show much. His big feather-horns at such times helped make him look like a ragged stub of a branch, or something else he wasn't. It is possible for a person to go very close to an owl without seeing him; and fortunately for Solomon, birds did not find him every day. For when they did, they mobbed him.

One day, rather late in the summer, Cock Robin found him and sent forth the alarm. To be sure, Solomon was doing no harm—just dozing, he was, on a branch. But Cock Robin scolded and sputtered and called him mean names; and the louder he talked, the more excited all the other birds in the neighborhood became. Before long there were twenty angry kingbirds and sparrows and other feather-folk, all threatening to do something terrible to Solomon.

Now, Solomon had been having a good comfortable nap, with his feathers all hanging loose, when Cock Robin chanced to alight on the branch near him. He pulled himself up very thin and as tall as possible, with his feathers drawn tight against his body. When the bird-mob got too near him, he looked at them with his big round eyes, and said, "Oh!" in a sweet high voice. But his soft tone did not turn away their wrath. They came at him harder than ever. Then Solomon showed his temper, for he was no coward. He puffed his feathers out till he looked big and round, and he snapped his beak till the click of it could be heard by his tormentors. And he hissed.

But twenty enemies were too many, and there was only one thing to be done. Solomon did it. First thing those birds knew, they were scolding at nothing at all; and way off in the darkest spot he could find in the woods, a little owl settled himself quite alone and listened while the din of a distant mob grew fainter and fainter and fainter, as one by one those twenty birds discovered that there was no one left on the branch to scold at.

If Solomon knew why the day birds bothered him so, he never told. He could usually keep out of their way in the shady woods in the summer; but in the winter, when the leaves were off all but the evergreen trees, he had fewer places to hide in. Of course, there were not then so many birds to worry him, for most of them went south for the snowy season. But Jay stayed through the coldest days and enjoyed every chance he had of pestering Solomon. I don't know that this was because he really disliked the little owl. Jay was as full of mischief as a crow, and if the world got to seeming a bit dull, instead of moping and feeling sorry and waiting for something to happen, Jay looked about for some way of amusing himself. He was something of a bully,—a great deal of a bully, in fact,—this dashing rascal in a gay blue coat; and the more he could swagger, the better he liked it.

He seemed, too, to have very much the same feeling that we mean by joy, in fun and frolic. There was, perhaps, in the sight of a bird asleep and listless in broad daylight, something amusing. He was in the habit of seeing the feather-folk scatter at his approach. If he understood why, that didn't bother him any. He was used to it, and there is no doubt he liked the power he had of making his fellow creatures fly around. When he found, sitting on a branch, with two toes front and two toes back, a downy puff with big round eyes and a Roman nose and feather-horns sticking up like the ears of a cat, maybe he was a bit puzzled because it didn't fly, too. Perhaps he didn't quite know what to make of poor little Solomon, who, disturbed from his nap, just drew himself up slim and tall, and remarked, "Oh!" in a sweet high voice.

But, puzzled or not, Jay knew very well what he could do about it. He had done it so many times before! It was a game he liked. He stood on a branch, and called Solomon names in loud, harsh tones. He flew around as if in a terrible temper, screaming at the top of his voice. When he began, there was not another day bird in sight. Before many minutes, all the chickadees, nuthatches, and woodpeckers within hearing had arrived, and had taken sides with Jay. Yes, even sunny-hearted Chick D.D. himself said things to Solomon that were almost saucy. I never heard that any of these mobs actually hurt our little friend; but they certainly disturbed his nap, and there was no peace for him until he slipped away. Where he went, there was no sound to tell, for his feathers were fringed with silent down. Perhaps some snow-bowed branch of evergreen gave him shelter, in a nook where he could see better than the day-eyed birds who tried to follow and then lost track of him.

So Solomon went on with his nap, and Jay started off in quest of other adventures. The winter air put a keen edge on his appetite, which was probably the reason why he began to hunt for some of the cupboards where food was stored. Of course, he had tucked a goodly supply of acorns and such things away for himself; but he slipped into one hollow in a tree that was well stocked with frozen fish, which he had certainly had no hand in catching. But what did it matter to the blue-jacketed robber if that fish had meant a three-night fishing at an air-hole in the ice? He didn't care (and probably didn't know) who caught it. It tasted good on a frosty day, so he feasted on fish in Solomon's pantry, while the little owl slept.

Well, if Jay, the bold dashing fellow, held noisy revel during the dazzling winter days, night came every once in so often; and then a quavering call, tremulous yet unafraid, told the listening world that an elf of the moonlight was claiming his own. And if some shivered at the sound, others there were who welcomed it as a challenge to enter the realm of a winter's night.

For, summer or winter, the night holds much of mystery, close to the heart of which lives a little downy owl, who wings his way silent as a shadow, whither he will. And when he calls, people who love the stars and the wonders they shine down upon sometimes go out to the woods and talk with him, for the words he speaks are not hard even for a human voice to say. There was once a boy, so a great poet tells us, who stood many a time at evening beneath the trees or by the glimmering lake, and called the owls that they might answer him. While he listened, who knows what the bird of wisdom told him about the night?

FOOTNOTES:

[3] *Hexapod Stories*, page 89.

XII
BOB THE VAGABOND

Bob had on his traveling suit, for a vagabond must go a-journeying. It would never do to stay too long in one place, and here it was August already. Why, he had been in Maine two months and more, and it is small wonder he was getting restless. Restless, though not unhappy! Bob was never that; for the joy of the open way was always before him, and whenever the impulse came, he could set sail and be off.

The meadows of Maine had been his choice for his honeymoon, and a glad time of it he and May had had with their snug little home of woven grass. That home was like an anchor to them both, and held their hearts fast during the days it had taken to make five grown-sized birds out of five eggs. But now that their sons and daughters were strong of wing and fully dressed in traveling suits like their mother's, it was well that Bob had put off his gay wedding clothes and donned a garb of about the same sort as that worn by the rest of his family; for dull colors are much the best for trips.

Now that they were properly dressed, there was nothing left to see to, except to join the Band of Bobolink Vagabonds. Of course no one can be a member of this band without the password; but there was nothing about that to worry Bob. When any of them came near, he called, "Chink," and the gathering flock would sing out a cheery "Chink" in reply: and that is the way he and his family were initiated into the Band of Bobolink Vagabonds. Anyone who can say "Chink" may join this merry company. That is, anyone who can pronounce it with just exactly the right sound!

So, with a flutter of pleasant excitement, they were gone. Off, they were, for a land that lies south of the Amazon, and with no more to say about it than, "Chink."

No trunk, no ticket, no lunch-box; and the land they would seek was four thousand miles or more away! Poor little Bob! had he but tapped at the door of Man with his farewell "Chink," someone could have let him see a map of his journey. For men have printed time-tables of the Bobolink Route, with maps to show what way it lies, and with the different Stations marked where food and rest can be found. The names of some of the most important Stations that a bobolink, starting from Maine, should stop at on the way to Brazil and Paraguay, are Maryland, South Carolina, Florida, Cuba, Jamaica, and Venezuela.

Does it seem a pity that the little ignorant bird started off without knowing even the name of one of these places? Ah, no! A journeying bobolink needs no advice. "Poor," indeed! Why, Bob had a gift that made him fortunate beyond the understanding of men. Nature has dealt generously with Man, to be sure, giving him power to build ships for the sea and the air, and trains for the land, whereon he may go, and power to print time-tables to guide the time of travel. But to Bob also, who could do none of these things, Nature had, nevertheless, been generous, and had given him power to go four thousand miles without losing his way, though he had neither chart nor compass. What it would be like to have this gift, we can hardly even guess—we who get lost in the woods a mile from home, and wander in bewildered circles, not knowing where to turn! We can no more know how Bob found his way than the born-deaf can know the sound of a merry tune, or the born-blind can know the look of a sunset sky. Some people think that, besides the five senses given to a man, Nature gave one more to the bobolink—a sixth gift, called a "sense of direction."

A wonderful gift for a vagabond! To journey hither and yon with never a fear of being lost! To go forty hundred miles and never miss the way! To sail over land and over sea,—over meadow and forest and mountain,—and reach the homeland, far south of the Amazon, at just the right time! To travel by starlight as well as by sunshine, without once mistaking the path!

By starlight? What, Bob, who had frolicked and chuckled through the bright June days, and dozed o' nights so quietly that never a passing owl could see a motion to tempt a chase?

Yes, when he joined the Band of Bobolink Vagabonds, the gates of the night, which had been closed to him by Sleep, were somehow thrown open, and Bob was free to journey, not only where he would, but when he would—neither darkness nor daylight having power to stop him then.

Is it strange that his wings quivered with the joy of voyaging as surely as the sails of a boat tighten in the tugging winds?

What would you give to see this miracle—a bobolink flying through the night? For it has been seen; there being men who go and watch, when their calendars tell them 't is time for birds to take their southward flight. Their eyes are too feeble to see such sights unaided; so they look through a telescope toward the full round moon, and then they can see the birds that pass between them and the light. Like a procession they go—the bobolinks and other migrants, too; for the night sky is filled with travelers when birds fly south.

But though we could not see them, we should know when they are on their way because of their voices. What would you give to hear this miracle—a bobolink calling his watchword through the night? For it has been heard; there being men who go to the hilltops and listen.

As they hear, now and again, wanderers far above them calling, "Chink," one to another, they know the bobolinks are on their way to a land that lies south of the Amazon, and that neither sleep nor darkness bars their path, which is open before them to take when and where they will.

And yet Bob and his comrades did not hasten. The year was long enough for pleasure by the way. He and May had worked busily to bring up a family of five fine sons and daughters early in the summer; and now that their children were able to look out for themselves, there was no reason why the birds should not have some idle, care-free hours.

It was time for the Feast of the Vagabonds.

Besides, it was time for the Feast of the Vagabonds, a ceremony that must be performed during the first weeks of the Migrant Flight; for it is a custom of the bobolinks, come down to them through no one knows how many centuries, to hold a farewell feast before leaving North America. If you will glance at a map of the Bobolink Route, you will see the names of the states they passed through. Our travelers did not know these names; but for all that, they found the Great Rice Trail and followed it. They found wild rice in the swamps of Maryland and the neighboring states. In South Carolina they found acres of cultivated rice. For rice is the favorite food during the Feast of the Vagabonds, and to them Nature has a special way of serving it. This same grain is eaten in many lands; taken in one way or another, it is said to be the principal food of about one half of all the people in the world. Bob didn't eat his in soup or pudding or chop-suey. He used neither spoon nor chop-sticks. He took his in the good old-fashioned way of his own folk—unripe, as most of us take our sweet corn, green and in the tender, milky stage, fresh from the stalk. He had been having a rather heavy meat diet in Maine, the meadow insects being abundant, and he relished the change. There was doubtless a good healthy reason for the ceremony of the Feast of the Vagabonds, as anyone who saw Bob may have guessed; for by the time he left South Carolina he was as fat as butter.

In following the Great Rice Trail, Bob went over the same road that he had taken the spring before when he was northward bound; but one could hardly believe him to be the same bird, for he looked different and he acted differently. In the late summer, the departing bird was dull of hue and, except for a few notes that once in a great while escaped him, like some nearly forgotten echo of the spring, he had no more music in him than his mate, May. And when they went southward, they went all together—the fathers and mothers and sons and daughters in one great company.

In the spring it had all been different: Bob had come north with his vagabond brothers a bit ahead of the sister-folk. And the vagabond brothers had been gay of garb—fresh black and white, with a touch of buff. And Bob and his band had been gay of voice. The flock of them had gathered in tree-tops and flooded the day with such mellow, laughing melodies as the world can have only in springtime—and only as long as the bobolinks last.

The ways of the springtime are for the spring, and those of the autumn for the fall of the year. So Bob, who, when northward bound a few months before, had taken part in the grand Festival of Song, now that he was southward bound, partook of the great Feast of the Vagabonds, giving himself whole-heartedly to each ceremony in turn, as a bobolink should, for such are the time-honored customs of his folk.

Honored for how long a time we do not know. Longer than the memory of man has known the rice-fields of South Carolina! Days long before that, when elephants trod upon that ground, did those great beasts hear the spring song of the bobolinks? Is the answer to that question buried in the rocks with the elephants? Bob didn't know. He flew over, with never a thought in his little head but for the Great Rice Trail leading him southward to Florida.

While there, some travelers would have gone about and watched men cut sponges, and have found out why Florida has a Spanish name. But not Bob! The Feast of the Vagabonds, which had lasted well-nigh all the way from Maryland, was still being observed, and even the stupidest person can see that rice is better to eat than sponges or history.

Then, as suddenly as if their "Chink, chink, chink" meant "One, two, three, away we go," the long feast was over, and their great flight again called them to wing their way into the night. How they found Cuba through the darkness, without knowing one star from another; what brought them to an island in the midst of the water that was everywhere alike—no man knows. But in Cuba they landed in good health and spirits. This was in September,—a very satisfactory time for a bird-visit,—and Bob and his comrades spent some little time there, it being October, indeed, when they arrived on the island of Jamaica. Now Jamaica, so people say who know the place, has a comfortable climate and thrilling views; but it didn't satisfy Bob. Not for long! Something south of the Amazon kept calling to him. Something that had called to his father and to his grandfather and to all his ancestors, ever since bobolinks first flew from North America to South America once every year.

How many ages this has been, who knows? Perhaps ever since the icy glaciers left Maine and made a chance for summer meadows there. Long, long, long, it has been, that something south of the Amazon has called to bobolinks and brought them on their way in the fall of the year. So the same impulse quickened Bob's heart that had stirred all his fathers, back through countless seasons. The same quiver for flight came to all the Band of Vagabonds. Was it homesickness? We do not know.

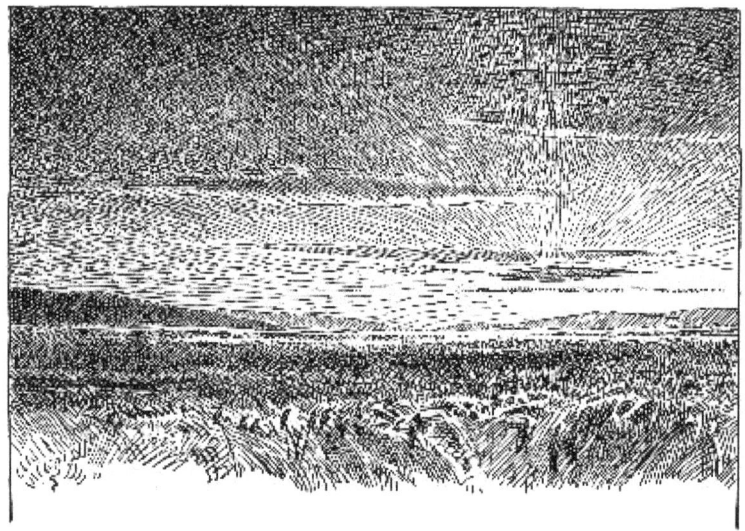

Something south of the Amazon kept calling to him.

We only know that a night came when Bob and his companions left the mountains of Jamaica below them and then behind them. Far, far behind them lay the island, and far, far ahead the coast they sought. Five hundred miles between Jamaica and a chance for rest or food. Five hundred miles; and the night lay about and above them and the waters lay underneath. The stars shone clear, but they knew not one from another. No guide, no pilot, no compass, such as we can understand, gave aid through the hours of their flight. But do you think they were afraid? Afraid of the dark, of the water, of the miles? Listen, in your fancy, and hear them call to one another. "Chink," they say; and though we do not know just what this means, we can tell from the sound that it is not a note of fear. And why fear? There was no storm to buffet them that night. They passed near no dazzling lighthouse, to bewilder them. No danger threatened, and something called them straight and steady on their way.

Oh, they were wonderful, that band! Perhaps among all living creatures of the world there is nothing more wonderful than a bird in his migrant flight—a bird whose blood is fresh with the air he breathes as only a bird can breathe; whose health is strong with the wholesome feast that he takes when and where he finds it; whose wings hold him in perfect flight through unweary miles; whose life is led, we know not how, on, on, on, and ever in the right direction.

Yes, Bob was wonderful when he flew from the mountains of Jamaica to the great savannas of Venezuela; but he made no fuss about it—seemed to feel no special pride. All he said was, "Chink," in the same matter-of-fact way that his bobolink forefathers had spoken, back through all the years when they, too, had taken this same flight over sea in the course of their vagabond journey.

From Venezuela to Paraguay there was no more ocean to cross, and there were frequent places for rest when Bob and his band desired. Groves there were, strange groves—some where Brazil nuts grew, and some where oranges were as common as apples in New England. There were chocolate trees and banana palms. There were pepper bushes, gay as our holly trees at Christmastime. Great flowering trees held out their blossom cups to brilliant hummingbirds hovering by hundreds all about them. Was there one among them with a ruby throat, like that of the hummingbird who feasted in the Cardinal-Flower Path near Peter Piper's home? Maybe 't was the self-same bird—who knows? And let's see—Peter Piper himself would be coming soon, would he not, to teeter and picnic along some pleasant Brazilian shore?

Perhaps Bob and Peter and the hummingbird, who had been summer neighbors in North America, would meet again now and then in that far south country. But I do not think they would know each other if they did. They had all seemed too busy with their own affairs to get acquainted.

Besides the groves where the nuts and fruit and flowers grew, the vagabonds passed over forests so dense and tangled that Bob caught never a glimpse of the monkeys playing there: big brown ones, with heads of hair that looked like wigs, and tiny white ones, timid and gentle, and other kinds, too, all of them being very wise in their wild ways—as wise, perhaps, as a hand-organ monkey, and much, much happier.

No, I don't think Bob saw the monkeys, but he must have caught glimpses of some members of the Parrot Family, for there were so many of them; and I'm sure he heard the racket they made when they talked together. One kind had feathers soft as the blue of a pale hyacinth flower, and a beak strong enough to crush nuts so hard-shelled that a man could not easily crack them with a hammer. But all that was as nothing to Bob. For 't was not grove or forest or beast or bird that the vagabonds were seeking.

When they had crossed the Amazon River, some of the band stopped in places that seemed inviting. But Bob and the rest of the company went on till they crossed the Paraguay River; and there, in the western part of that country, they made themselves at home. A strange, topsy-turvy land it is— as queer in some ways as the Wonderland Alice entered when she went through the Looking-Glass; for in Paraguay January comes in the middle of summer; and the hot, muggy winds blow from the north; and the cool, refreshing breezes come from the south; and some of the wood is so heavy that it will not float in water; and the people make tea with dried holly leaves! But to the Band of Vagabond Bobolinks it was not topsy-turvy, for it was home; and they found the Paraguay prairies as well suited to the comforts of their January summer as the meadows of the North had been for their summer of June.

Bob was satisfied. He had flown four thousand miles from a meadow and had found a prairie! And if, in all that wonderful journey, he had not paid over much attention to anything along the way except swamps and marshes, do not scorn him for that. Remember always that Bob *found* his prairie and that Peter *found* his shore.

It is somewhere written, "Seek and ye shall find." 'Tis so with the children of birds—they find what Nature has given them to seek. And is it so with the children of men? Never think that Nature has been less kind to boys and girls than to birds. Unto Bob was given the fields to seek, and he had no other choice. Unto Peter the shores, and that was all. But unto us is given a chance to choose what we will seek. If it is as far away as the prairies of Paraguay, shall we let a dauntless little vagabond put our faith to shame? If it is as near as our next-door meadow, shall we not find a full measure of happiness there—mixed with the bobolink's music of June?

Nature has kept faith with him and brought him safely back to his meadow.

For Bob comes back to the North again, bringing with him springtime melodies, which poets sing about but no human voice can mimic. Bob, who has dusted the dull tips from his feathers as he flew, and who, garbed for the brightness of our June, makes a joyful sound; for Nature has kept faith with him and brought him safely back to his meadow, though the journey from and to it numbered eight thousand miles!

His trail is the open lane of the air,
And the winds, they call him everywhere;
So he wings him North, dear burbling Bob,
With throat aquiver and heart athrob;
And he sings o' joy in the month of June
Enough to keep the year in tune.

Then, when the rollicking young of his kind
Yearn for the paths that the vagabonds find,
He leads them out over loitering ways

Where the Southland beckons with luring days;
To wait till the laughter-like lilt of his song
Is ripe for the North again—missing him long!

NOTES

CONSERVATION

We cannot read much nature literature of the present day without coming upon a plea, either implied or expressed, for "conservation." Even the child will wish to know—and there is grave need that he should know—why many people, and societies of people, are trying to save what it has so long been the common custom to waste. Boys and girls living in the Eastern States will be interested to know who is Ornithologist to the Massachusetts State Board of Agriculture, and what his duties are; those in the West will like to know why a publication called "California Fish and Game" should have for its motto, "Conservation of Wild Life through Education"; those between the East and the West will like to learn what is being done in their own states for bird or beast or blossom.

Fortunately the idea is not hard to grasp. Conservation is really but doing unto others as we would that others should do unto us—so living that other life also may have a fair chance. It was a child who wrote, from her understanding heart:—

"When I do have hungry feels I feel the hungry feels the birds must be having. So I do have comes to tie things on the trees for them. Some have likes for different things. Little gray one of the black cap has likes for suet. And other folks has likes for other things."—From *The Story of Opal*.

CHICK, D.D.

Penthestes atricapillus is the name men have given the bird who calls himself the "Chickadee."

The Bird (Beebe), page 186. "The next time you see a wee chickadee, calling contentedly and happily while the air makes you shiver from head to foot, think of the hard-shelled frozen insects passing down his throat, the icy air entering lungs and air-sacs, and ponder a moment on the wondrous little laboratory concealed in his mite of a body, which his wings bear up with so little effort, which his tiny legs support, now hopping along a branch, now suspended from some wormy twig.

"Can we do aught but silently marvel at this alchemy? A little bundle of muscle and blood, which in this freezing weather can transmute frozen beetles and zero air into a happy, cheery little Black-capped Chickadee, as he names himself, whose trustfulness warms our hearts!

"And the next time you raise your gun to needlessly take a feathered life, think of the marvellous little engine which your lead will stifle forever; lower your weapon and look into the clear bright eyes of the bird whose body equals yours in physical perfection, and whose tiny brain can generate a sympathy, a love for its mate, which in sincerity and unselfishness suffers little when compared with human affection."

Bird Studies with a Camera (Chapman), pages 47-61.

Handbook of Nature-Study (Comstock), pages 66-68.

Nature Songs and Stories (Creighton), pages 3-5.

American Birds (Finley), pages 15-22.

Winter (Sharp), chapter VI.

Educational Leaflet No. 61. (National Association of Audubon Societies.)

This story was first published in the *Progressive Teacher*, December, 1920.

THE FIVE WORLDS OF LARIE

Larus argentatus, the Herring Gull.

Larie's "policeman," like Ardea's "soldier," is usually called a "warden." No thoughtful or informed person can look upon "bird study" as merely a pleasant pastime for children and a harmless fad for the outdoor man and woman. It is a matter that touches, not only the æsthetic, but the economic welfare of the country: a matter that has concern for legislators and presidents as well as for naturalists. In this connection it is helpful to read some such discussion as is given in the first four references.

Bird Study Book (Pearson), pages 101-213; 200.

Birds in their Relation to Man (Weed and Dearborn), pages 255-330.

Bird-Lore, vol. 22, pages 376-380.

Useful Birds and their Protection (Forbush), pages 354-421.

Birds of Ohio (Dawson), pages 548-551; "Herring Gull."

Bird Book (Eckstorm), pages 23-29; "The Herring Gull."

American Birds (Finley), pages 211-217; "Gull Habits."

Game-Laws for 1920 (Lawyer and Earnshaw), pages 68-75; "Migratory-Bird Treaty Act."

Tales from Birdland (Pearson), pages 3-27; "Hardheart, the Gull."

Educational Leaflet No. 29; "The Herring Gull." (National Association of Audubon Societies.)

PETER PIPER

Actitis macularia, the Spotted Sandpiper.

Educational Leaflet No. 51. (National Association of Audubon Societies.)

"A leisurely little flight to Brazil."

Peter, the gypsy, and Bob, the vagabond, are both famous travelers, and might have passed each other on the way, coming and going, in Venezuela and in Brazil. Peter, like Bob, is a night migrant, stopping in the daytime for rest and food.

For references to literature on bird-migration, the list under the notes to "Bob, the Vagabond," may be used.

GAVIA OF IMMER LAKE

Gavia immer, the Loon.

The Bird (Beebe). "Hesperornis—a wingless, toothed, diving bird, about 5 feet in length, which inhabited the great seas during the Cretaceous period, some four millions of years ago." (Legend under colored frontispiece.)

Life Histories of North American Diving Birds (Bent), pages 47-60.

Bird Book (Eckstorm), pages 9-13.

By-Ways and Bird-Notes (Thompson), pages 170-71. "The cretaceous birds of America all appear to be aquatic, and comprise some eight or a dozen genera, and many species. Professor Marsh and others have found in Kansas a large number of most interesting fossil birds, one of them, a gigantic loon-like creature, six feet in length from beak to toe, taken from the yellow chalk of the Smoky Hill River region and from calcareous shale near Fort Wallace, is named *Hesperornis regalis*."

Educational Leaflet No. 78. (National Association of Audubon Societies.)

If twenty years of undisputed possession seems long enough to give a man a legal title to "his" land, surely birds have a claim too ancient to be ignored by modern beings. Are we not in honor bound to share what we have so recently considered "ours," with the creatures that inherited the earth before the coming of their worst enemy, Civilization? And in so far as lies within our power, shall we not protect the free, wild feathered folk from ourselves?

EVE AND PETRO

Petrochelidon lunifrons, Cliff-Swallow, Eave-Swallow.

Bird Studies with a Camera (Chapman), pages 89-105; "Where Swallows Roost."

Handbook of Nature-Study (Comstock), pages 112-113.

Bird Migration (Cooke), pages 5, 9, 19-20, 26, 27; Fig. 6.

Our Greatest Travelers (Cooke), page 349; "Migration Route of the Cliff Swallows."

Bird Book (Eckstorm), pages 201-12.

Bird-Lore, vol. 21, page 175; "Helping Barn and Cliff Swallows to Nest."

UNCLE SAM

Haliæetus leucocephalus, the Bald Eagle.

Stories of Bird Life (Pearson), pages 71-80; "A Pair of Eagles."

The Fall of the Year (Sharp), chapter V.

Educational Leaflet No. 82. (National Association of Audubon Societies.)

At the time this story goes to press, our national emblem is threatened with extermination. The following references indicate the situation in 1920:—

Conservationist, The, vol. 3, pages 60-61; "Our National Emblem."

National Geographic Magazine, vol. 38, page 466.

Natural History, vol. 20, pages 259 and 334; "The Dead Eagles of Alaska now number 8356."

Science, vol. 50, pages 81-84; "Zoölogical Aims and Opportunities," by Willard G. Van Name.

CORBIE

Corvus brachyrhynchos, the Crow.

The Bird (Beebe), pages 153, 158, 172, 200-01, 209. "When the brain of a bird is compared with that of a mammal, there is seen to be a conspicuous difference, since the outer surface is perfectly smooth in birds, but is wound about in convolutions in the higher four-footed animals. This latter condition is said to indicate a greater degree of intelligence; but when we look at the brain of a young musk-ox or walrus, and find convolutions as deep as those of a five-year-old child, and when we compare the wonderfully varied life of birds, and realize what resource and intelligence they frequently display in adapting themselves to new or untried conditions, a smooth brain does not seem such an inferior organ as is often inferred by writers on the subject. I would willingly match a crow against a walrus any day in a test of intelligent behavior.... A crow... though with horny, shapeless lips, nose, and mouth, looks at us through eyes so expressive, so human, that no wonder man's love has gone out to feathered creatures throughout all his life on the earth."

Handbook of Nature-Study (Comstock), pages 129-32.

American Birds (Finley), pages 69-77; "Jack Crow."

The Crow and its Relation to Man (Kalmbach).

Outdoor Studies (Needham), pages 47-53; "Not so Black as he is Painted."

Tales from Birdland (Pearson), pages 128-52; "Jim Crow of Cow Heaven."

Our Backdoor Neighbors (Pellett), pages 181-98; "A Jolly Old Crow."

Our Birds and their Nestlings (Walker), pages 76-85; "The Children of a Crow."

The Story of Opal (Whiteley); "Lars Porsena."

Gray Lady and the Birds (Wright), pages 114-28.

Bird Lore, vol. 22 (1919), pages 203-04; "A Nation-Wide Effort to Destroy Crows."

Educational Leaflet No. 77. (National Association of Audubon Societies.)

ARDEA'S SOLDIER

Ardea's scientific name used to be *Ardea candidissima*, and the older references to this bird will be found under that name, though at present it is known as *Egretta candidissima*. It is commonly called the Snowy Egret, or the Snowy Heron. The other white heron wearing "aigrettes" is *Herodias egretta*. Ardea's "soldier," like Larie's "policeman," is usually spoken of as a "warden." With reference to this story there is much of interest in the following:—

Bird Study Book (Pearson), pages 140-66, "The Traffic in Feathers"; pages 167-89, "Bird Protection Laws"; pages 190-213, "Bird Reservations": pages 244-58, "Junior Audubon Classes."

Stories of Bird Life (Pearson), pages 153-60; "Levy, the Story of an Egret."

Birds in their Relation to Man (Weed and Dearborn), pages 237-38.

Gray Lady and the Birds (Wright), pages 67-80; "Feathers and Hats."

Educational Leaflets Nos. 54 and 54A; "The Egret" and "The Snowy Egret." (National Association of Audubon Societies.)

To Mr. T. Gilbert Pearson, who has visited more egret colonies than any other person in the country, and who, in leading fights for their protection, has kept in very close touch with the egret situation, an expression of indebtedness and appreciation is due for his kindness in reading "Ardea's Soldier" while yet in manuscript, and for certain suggestions with reference to the story.

THE FLYING CLOWN

Chordeiles virginianus, the Nighthawk or Bull-bat.

Bird Migration (Cooke), pages 5, 7, 9.

Nature Sketches in Temperate America (Hancock), pages 246-48.

Birds in their Relation to Man (Weed and Dearborn), pages 178-80.

Bird-Lore, vol. 20 (1918), page 285.

Educational Leaflet No. 1. (National Association of Audubon Societies.)

THE LOST DOVE

Ectopistes migratorius, the Passenger Pigeon.

"How can a billion doves be lost?"

History of North American Birds (Baird, Brewer and Ridgway), vol. 3, pages 368-74.

Michigan Bird Life (Barrows), pages 238-51.

Birds that Hunt and are Hunted (Blanchan), pages 294-96.

Travels of Birds (Chapman), pages 73-74.

Birds of Ohio (Dawson and Jones), pages 425-27.

Passenger Pigeon (Mershon).

Natural History of the Farm (Needham), pages 114-15. "The wild pigeon was the first of our fine game birds to disappear. Its social habits were its undoing, when once guns were brought to its pursuit. It flew in great flocks, which were conspicuous and noisy, and which the hunter could follow by eye and ear, and mow down with shot at every resting-place. One generation of Americans found pigeons in 'inexhaustible supply'; the next saw them vanish—vanish so quickly, that few museums even sought to keep specimens of their skins or their nests or their eggs; the third generation (which we represent) marvels at the true tales of their aforetime abundance, and at the swiftness of their passing; and it allows the process of extermination to go on only a little more slowly with other fine native species."

Bird Study Book (Pearson), pages 128-29. "Passenger Pigeons as late as 1870 were frequently seen in enormous flocks. Their numbers during the periods of migration were one of the greatest ornithological wonders of the world. Now the birds are gone. What is supposed to have been the last one died in captivity in the Zoölogical Park of Cincinnati, at 2 P.M. on the afternoon of September 1, 1914. Despite the generally accepted statement that these birds succumbed to the guns, snares, and nets of hunters, there is a second cause, which doubtless had its effect in hastening the disappearance of the species. The cutting away of vast forests, where the birds were accustomed to gather and feed on mast, greatly restricted their feeding range. They collected in enormous colonies for the purpose of rearing their young; and after the forests of the Northern states were so largely destroyed, the birds seem to have been driven far up into Canada, quite beyond their usual breeding range. Here, as Forbush suggests, the summer probably was not sufficiently long to enable them to rear their young successfully."

Birds in their Relation to Man (Weed and Dearborn), pages 219-22.

Educational Leaflet No. 6. (National Association of Audubon Societies.) "Those who study with care the history of the extermination of the Pigeons will see, however, that all the theories brought forward to account for the destruction of the birds by other causes than man's agency are wholly inadequate. There was but one cause for the diminution of the birds, which was widespread, annual, perennial, continuous, and enormously destructive—their persecution by mankind. Every great nesting-ground was besieged by a host of people as soon as it was discovered, many of them professional pigeoners, armed with all the most effective engines of slaughter known. Many times the birds were so persecuted that they finally left their young to the mercies of the pigeoners; and even when they remained, most of the young were killed and sent to the market, and the hosts of the adults were decimated."

LITTLE SOLOMON OTUS

Otus asio, the Screech Owl, are the scientific and common names of our little friend Solomon. Perhaps the fact that owls stand upright and gaze at one with both eyes to the front, accounts in part for their looking so wise that they have been used as a symbol of wisdom for many centuries.

In the Library of Congress in Washington, there is a picture called "The Boy of Winander." When looking at this, or some copy of it, it is pleasant to remember the lines of Wordsworth's poem:—

There was a Boy; ye knew him well, ye cliffs
And islands of Winander!—many a time,
At evening, when the earliest stars began
To move along the edges of the hills,
Rising or setting, would he stand alone,
Beneath the trees, or by the glimmering lake;
And there, with fingers interwoven, both hands
Pressed closely palm to palm and to his mouth
Uplifted, he, as through an instrument,
Blew music hootings to the silent owls,
That they might answer him.

Following are a few references to Screech Owls:—

Handbook of Nature-Study (Comstock), pages 104-07.

Some Common Game, Aquatic and Rapacious Birds (McAtee and Beal), pages 27-28.

Our Backdoor Neighbors (Pellet), pages 63-74; "The Neighborly Screech Owls."

My Pets (Saunders), pages 11-33.

Birds in their Relation to Man (Weed and Dearborn), page 199.

Educational Leaflet No. 11. (National Association of Audubon Societies.)

BOB, THE VAGABOND

Dolichonyx oryzivorus, the Bobolink.

Educational Leaflet No. 38. (National Association of Audubon Societies.)

The Bobolink Route

Maps, showing the route of migrant bobolinks may be found in *Bird Migration* (Cooke), page 6;

Our Greatest Travelers (Cooke), page 365.

Other interesting accounts of bird-migrations may be found in *Travels of Birds* (Chapman).

Bird Study Book (Pearson), chapter IV.

History tells us when Columbus discovered Cuba and when Sebastian Cabot sailed up the Paraguay River; but when bobolinks discovered that island, or first crossed that river, no man can ever know. The physical perfection that permits such journeys as birds take is cause for admiration. In this connection much of interest will be found in

The Bird (Beebe), chapter VII, "The Breath of a Bird," from which we make a brief quotation. "Birds require, comparatively, a vastly greater strength and 'wind' in traversing such a thin, unsupporting medium as air than animals need for terrestrial locomotion. Even more wonderful than mere flight is the performance of a bird when it springs from the ground, and goes circling upward higher and higher on rapidly beating wings, all the while pouring forth a continuous series of musical notes.... A human singer is compelled to put forth all his energy in his vocal efforts; and if, while singing, he should start on a run even on level ground, he Would become exhausted at once.... The average person uses only about one seventh of his lung capacity in ordinary breathing, the rest of the air remaining at the bottom of the lung, being termed 'residual.' As this is vitiated by its stay in the lung, it does harm rather than good by its presence.... As we have seen, the lungs of a bird are small and non-elastic, but this is more than compensated by the continuous passage of fresh air, passing not only into but entirely *through* the lungs into the air-sacs, giving, therefore, the very best chance for oxygenation to take place in every portion of the lungs. When we compare the estimated number of breaths which birds and men take in a minute,—thirteen to sixteen in the latter, twenty to sixty in birds,—we realize better how birds can perform such wonderful feats of song and flight."

Milton Keynes UK
Ingram Content Group UK Ltd.
UKHW040900050124
435493UK00006B/968